Praise for *YouTube for Business*

"Be on the forefront of modern marketing using YouTube. Miller's book provides a comprehensive reference that any small business owner can understand and implement.

This is the must-have, small business book of the year for any business interested in marketing on the Internet. Miller tells you everything you need to know about how to use YouTube as part of your marketing strategy.

Everything you need to know to get the marketing message for your small business heard in a very modern, economical way.

Miller has written a comprehensive guide to using YouTube as part of your marketing mix. This book is essential to any small business looking to make a big impact on a limited budget."

—Judith Kautz, Editor, Small Business Notes

"If you're looking for ways to promote your business, you can't get much more effective than YouTube—and this book is the must-have tool for doing just that."

—Wendy Boswell, Editor, About Web Search

No matt   *6/09*   el Miller's
YouTube   ing YouTube
into you   for granted
and cl   day's business w   enced digital m

Dummies

Wow!   things
like h   even
more   ven in-
depth   to
YouTu

—Sc   he Virtual
                                                      Economy"

YouTube® for Business

Online Video Marketing for Any Business

Michael Miller

 800 East 96th Street,
Indianapolis, Indiana 46240 USA

YouTube® for Business: Online Video Marketing for Any Business

Copyright © 2009 by Pearson Education, Inc.

ISBN-13: 978-0-7897-3797-7
ISBN-10: 0-7897-3797-3

Library of Congress Cataloging-in-Publication Data

Miller, Michael, 1958-

  YouTube for business : online video marketing for any business / Michael Miller.

    p. cm.

  Includes index.

  ISBN 978-0-7897-3797-7

  1. Internet marketing. 2. Webcasting. 3. YouTube (Firm) I. Title.

  HF5415.1265.M556 2009

  658.8'72--dc22

                                2008028344

Printed in the United States of America

Second Printing: October 2008

Trademarks

Warning and Disclaimer

Bulk Sales

Que Publishing offers excellent discounts on this book when ordered in quantity for bulk purchases or special sales. For more information, please contact

   U.S. Corporate and Government Sales

   1-800-382-3419

   corpsales@pearsontechgroup.com

For sales outside of the U.S., please contact

   International Sales

   international@pearson.com

Associate Publisher
Greg Wiegand

Acquisitions Editor
Michelle Newcomb

Development Editor
Kevin Howard

Managing Editor
Patrick Kanouse

Project Editor
Mandie Frank

Copy Editor
Mike Henry

Indexer
Brad Herriman

Technical Editor
John Rice

Publishing Coordinator
Cindy Teeters

Designer
Anne Jones

Composition
Bronkella Publishing

Contents at a Glance

Table of Contents

About the Author

Michael Miller is a successful and prolific author. He is known for his casual, easy-to-read writing style and his ability to explain a wide variety of complex topics to an everyday audience.

Mr. Miller has written more than 80 nonfiction books over the past two decades, with more than a million copies in print. His books for Que include *YouTube 4 You*, *Making a Living from Your eBay Business*, *Tricks of the eBay Business Masters*, and *Googlepedia: The Ultimate Google Resource*.

You can email Mr. Miller directly at youtube4business@molehillgroup.com. His website is at www.molehillgroup.com, his YouTube channel is at www.youtube.com/user/trapperjohn2000, and his Video Blogging for Business video blog is at businessvideoblog.blogspot.com.

Dedication

To Sherry. It's even better now.

Acknowledgments

Thanks to the usual suspects at Que, including but not limited to Greg Wiegand, Michelle Newcomb, Kevin Howard, Mike Henry, Mandie Frank, and technical editor John Rice.

We Want to Hear from You!

As the reader of this book, *you* are our most important critic and commentator. We value your opinion and want to know what we're doing right, what we could do better, what areas you'd like to see us publish in, and any other words of wisdom you're willing to pass our way.

As an associate publisher for Que Publishing, I welcome your comments. You can email or write me directly to let me know what you did or didn't like about this book—as well as what we can do to make our books better.

Please note that I cannot help you with technical problems related to the topic of this book. We do have a User Services group, however, where I will forward specific technical questions related to the book.

When you write, please be sure to include this book's title and author as well as your name, email address, and phone number. I will carefully review your comments and share them with the author and editors who worked on the book.

Email: feedback@quepublishing.com

Mail: Greg Wiegand
         Associate Publisher
         Que Publishing
         800 East 96th Street
         Indianapolis, IN 46240 USA

Reader Services

Visit our website and register this book at www.informit.com/title/ 9780789737977 for convenient access to any updates, downloads, or errata that might be available for this book.

Introduction

Unless you've been living in a cave for the past year or two, you've no doubt heard of YouTube, the video-sharing site owned by Google. YouTube lets anyone post videos online that everyone can watch. It's a fun site and a popular one, constantly ranking in the top ten of all sites on the Web with close to 20 million visitors per month. With more than 100 million videos on the YouTube site (more than 80% being amateur in nature), it would take a viewer more than 400 years to watch them all!

For businesses, YouTube represents a new and exciting way to reach potential customers. But how do you market to YouTube's 20 million viewers? It's surprisingly easy—if you know the secrets.

That's why I wrote this book. I designed *YouTube for Business: Online Video Marketing for Any Business* to help any business, small or large, incorporate YouTube as a part of its online marketing mix. You learn how YouTube can help you market your company, brand, products, and services online; what types of videos you should create; how to create those videos; and how to promote and make money from your YouTube videos. It's easy enough that any business can do it.

The information included in this book is both strategic and technical. That means you find general marketing advice alongside specific technical instructions; you learn how to use YouTube as a marketing tool as well as how to create, post, and manage YouTube-friendly videos. If you do it right, YouTube can become an important part of your marketing mix and drive a lot of traffic (and sales) to your existing website.

If you don't believe me, just look at the five businesses profiled throughout this book. Some are large and some are small, but all get tremendous value from a minimal investment. Read how they do it and learn from their experiences.

How This Book Is Organized

YouTube for Business: Online Video Marketing for Any Business is part marketing text, part computer book; that's because you need both marketing and technical skills to take best advantage of YouTube as a marketing channel. To that end, I organized this book into five main parts, as follows:

- **Part I, "Marketing Your Business Online with YouTube,"** helps you incorporate YouTube as part of your online marketing strategy. You learn how YouTube can help you market your business, as well as get advice on how to create more effective YouTube videos.

- **Part II, "Producing Your YouTube Videos,"** is all about the technical aspect of creating videos for online videos. You learn the necessary audio and video technology, as well as how to create webcam, semi-pro, and professional videos. You even learn how to edit your videos by using any desktop personal computer.

- **Part III, "Managing Your YouTube Videos,"** shows you how to upload your videos to the YouTube site, create a presence in the YouTube community, and incorporate your YouTube videos into your own website.

- **Part IV, "Working with YouTube Video Blogs,"** covers a specific type of YouTube video: the video blog or *vlog*. You learn how to create and manage your own video blog, as well as how to integrate your video blog with an existing text-based blog.

- **Part V, "Promotion and Monetization,"** is all about the money. You learn how to track your videos' performance, how to promote your YouTube videos, and how to generate revenues from your videos.

And, as I mentioned previously, each section ends with a profile of a successful business using YouTube as part of its marketing mix. These case studies show you exactly how businesses just like yours use YouTube; there's real value in these real-world examples.

Conventions Used in This Book

I hope that this book is easy enough to figure out on its own, without requiring its own instruction manual. As you read through the pages, however, it helps to know precisely how I've presented specific types of information.

Web Pages

Obviously, there are a lot of web page addresses in the book, like this one: www.youtube.com. When you see a web page address (also known as a *URL* or *uniform resource locator*), you can go to that web page by entering the URL into the address box in your web browser. I've made every effort to ensure the accuracy of the web addresses presented here, but given the ever-changing nature of the Web, don't be surprised if you run across an address or two that's changed. I apologize in advance.

Special Elements

As you read through this book, you'll note several special elements, presented in what we in the publishing business call *margin notes*. There are different types of margin notes for different types of information, as you see here.

note

This is a note that presents some interesting information, even if it isn't wholly relevant to the discussion in the main text.

tip

This is a tip that might prove useful for whatever it is you're in the process of doing.

caution

This is a warning that something you might accidentally do might have undesirable results—so take care!

There's More Online

This book has its own collection of YouTube videos and a video blog. You can find my YouTube videos on my channel page, located at www.youtube.com/user/trapperjohn2000. The *Video Blogging for Business* video blog is at businessvideoblog.blogspot.com.

The videos on my vlog and YouTube channel demonstrate many of the essential techniques and approaches discussed in this book that are best shown in video format. The video blog also links to videos from other businesses currently using YouTube for promotion and marketing.

Together, these videos provide a welcome supplement to the text-based material presented in this book. I recommend that you check them out.

And, while you're online, you might want to browse over to my personal website, located at www.molehillgroup.com. Here you'll find more information on this book and other books I've written—including an errata page for this book, in the inevitable event that an error or two creeps into this text. (Hey, nobody's perfect!)

In addition, know that I love to hear from readers of my books. If you want to contact me, feel free to email me at youtube4business@ molehillgroup.com. I can't promise that I'll answer every message, but I do promise that I'll read each one!

Get Ready to YouTube

Now that you know how to use this book, it's time to get to the heart of the matter. To learn more about YouTube, and how to make it an essential part of your online marketing mix, get ready and turn the page!

Marketing Your Business Online with YouTube

1

How YouTube Can Help You Market Your Business

YouTube is a site where you can watch just about any type of video imaginable. There are videos of cute kittens, indie rock bands, standup comedy routines, stupid human tricks, vintage television commercials, high school musicals, film school projects, home movies, breaking news clips, personal video blogs—you name it. Users have uploaded literally millions of video clips, and everyone can watch them in their web browser at no cost.

Most of the videos on YouTube are amateurish, produced by non-professionals with simple webcams or consumer camcorders. But within the mix are an increasing number of more professional clips, designed to promote a particular product or business.

That's right: Businesses small and large have discovered YouTube. In fact, YouTube is the hottest new medium for online marketing; if your business has an online component, you could, and should, be promoting it via YouTube videos.

A Short History of YouTube

If you've never visited the YouTube website (shown in Figure 1.1), you've missed out on the hottest thing on the Internet today. In fact, YouTube has become so pervasive and so innovative that *Time* magazine named it Invention of the Year in 2006—which is pretty good for a site that came to life only the year before.

FIGURE 1.1

The YouTube site—home base for all your online video marketing.

YouTube: The Early Days

YouTube was the brainchild of three former PayPal employees: Chad Hurley, Steven Chen, and Jawed Karim. The three founders had left their former company and were looking for a new business opportunity. After exploring a few less interesting ideas, they eventually realized there was a real need for a service that facilitated the process of uploading, watching, and sharing videos. Hence the development of YouTube.

The trio registered the domain name YouTube.com on February 15, 2005 and then started developing the technology for the site—in Hurley's garage. Chen, the programmer of the bunch, worked with Adobe's Flash development language to stream video clips inside a web browser. Hurley, a user interface expert, adopted the concept of *tags* to let users identify and share the videos they liked. Together they came up with a way to let users paste video clips onto their own web pages, which expanded the reach of the site.

The development work done, a public beta test version of the site went live in May 2005. After a few months of working out the kinks of the site, the three men officially launched YouTube in December 2005.

YouTube Launches—And Gets Acquired

YouTube proved immensely popular from virtually the first day in business. Site traffic that first month was three million visitors, which is pretty good for a startup. The number of visitors tripled by the third month (February), tripled again by July (to 30 million visitors), and reached 38 million visitors by the end of the site's first year in business. That made YouTube one of the top 10 sites on the Web, period—and one of the fastest growing websites in history.

That kind of growth didn't go unnoticed, especially by competing websites. The biggest of the competing sites, Google, set out to buy the company, and did so in October 2006. Google paid $1.65 billion for YouTube—an incredible sum for such a young company, and one that had yet to generate significant revenues.

This put YouTube smack in the middle of the mighty Google empire. That said, YouTube continues to operate independently of the mother ship; the site looks and acts pretty much the same today as it did in the pre-Google days. The only big difference is volume. The number of videos and users on the site continue to grow, which is great for businesses looking to take advantage of the opportunity.

YouTube Today

How big is YouTube today? According to the market research firm comScore, YouTube consistently rates in the top five of all websites, with close to 80 million visitors per month. And those visitors are watching a lot of videos—more than three billion videos a month, or a third of all the videos viewed on the Web.

Not surprisingly, it appears that YouTube is replacing traditional television viewing for many users. According to Google, an average YouTube viewer spends 164 minutes online everyday; in contrast, viewers spend just 130 minutes per day watching traditional television. Where would you rather put your marketing message?

Is Video Right for Your Business?

Large businesses have long embraced video marketing in the form of traditional television advertising. But television ads were outside the purview of smaller businesses unless they could afford a late night spot on a local channel.

Thanks to YouTube, however, businesses both large and small can effectively market themselves via online videos. The cost of posting a video to the YouTube site is zero; the only cost is the expense of shooting and editing the video. This makes YouTube marketing affordable for virtually any business.

But is video the right way to promote your business? If you've never produced a video or television ad, you might not be sure. But in many cases, a short video can have a tremendous positive effect on your website's traffic or in orders generated via an 800-number.

Let's face it: Consumers love to watch videos. We're becoming less a society of readers and more one of watchers; the average consumer would rather watch a video than read a text-based advertisement. Like it or not, you need to be aware of and adapt your marketing mix to this trend.

And here's the thing: The more interesting the video, the bigger the audience it will attract. You can include a lot of information in a short three-minute video, and you can present that information in an entertaining and engaging fashion. People like to be entertained, educated, and informed, and online video can do all three things—and, in the process, provide a clear picture of the product or service you're offering.

DoubleClick conducted a survey in 2006 that codified the benefits of online video advertising. Here's what it found:

- A high percentage of audiences interact with video ads, via mouseovers, use of the video control buttons, and so forth.

- Viewers click the Play button in video ads twice as often as they click traditional image ads. In addition, click-through rates are four to five times higher than with traditional text or image ads.

- Viewers actually watch video ads. On average, video ads play two-thirds of the way through.

Here's how Rick Bruner, research director at DoubleClick, assessed the results:

Online video ads are quickly becoming the medium of choice to drive both brand awareness and sales. The results show that there are clear ROI advantages to placing video ads. We expect to see strong growth in the number of companies reaping the benefits of online video advertising in the coming months and years.

Done effectively, a YouTube video can add a viral component to your company's website. You see, when you post a video to YouTube, that video takes on a life of its own. It will be viewed by thousands of YouTube users, posted to numerous websites and blogs, emailed around the Internet—you name it. Just make sure you tailor your message to the YouTube crowd, and you can start generating traffic from the millions of people who frequent YouTube each day. Any user watching your video is now a potential customer—assuming that you include your website's address or other contact information in the video.

What Types of Businesses Can Use YouTube?

It doesn't matter what type of business you run or how large that business is. You can create effective videos that will attract YouTube viewers and drive more business to your website or 800-number. All types of businesses are getting into the YouTube scene: local businesses, major national marketers, ad agencies, real estate agencies, consultants and motivational speakers, Internet-only retailers—you name it.

For example, Nike (www.youtube.com/user/Nikesoccer) enlisted Brazilian soccer star Ronaldinho to produce a gritty clip that the company then uploaded to the YouTube site. Word-of-mouth quickly built, and YouTube viewers started to email the video to friends and embed it in their blogs and MySpace/Facebook pages. The video was viewed more than 3 million times; all that exposure cost Nike next to nothing to produce—and absolutely nothing to distribute.

Of course, you don't need to be a big company like Nike to benefit from YouTube marketing. Take, as another example, A-Cappella.com, an Internet retailer of CDs, DVDs, sheet music, and books for unaccompanied (a cappella) singing groups. During the 2007 holiday season, a video of Indiana University's Straight No Chaser vocal group took off on YouTube, registering 400,000 views per day. Captivated viewers found A-Cappella.com, which offered a DVD of the group's performance. The company, which normally handled about 60 orders per day, suddenly found itself swamped with orders—eventually selling more than 5,300 copies of the group's DVD. And it all happened without spending a penny on advertising.

Other companies, large and small, have benefited from the exposure of YouTube videos. H&R Block, Intuit, Levi's, Mountain Dew, MTV, Smirnoff, and Warner Brothers are just a few of the recognizable names promoting their products and brands on YouTube; hundreds of smaller companies are also making YouTube part of their marketing mix.

Companies of all types market on YouTube. Movie studios and record labels were some of the first to jump on the YouTube bandwagon, but you can find videos from companies in all manner of industries, from travel agencies to pottery shops to real estate agencies. If what you're selling is in any way visual, which almost everything is, YouTube is a perfect medium for your company's advertising message.

What Kinds of Videos Can You Produce?

What types of videos do companies use to market their products and services on YouTube? There's a lot of variety, depending on the type of business or product marketed. You can find everything from television commercials, movie trailers, and infomercials to product demonstrations, video blogs, and real estate walk-throughs.

The key is to offer a video that YouTube users actually want to watch. That means a video that has some sort of entertainment, educational, or informational value. In other words, your video needs to entertain, educate, or inform—or no one will watch it.

Inform and Sell

One way to do this is to create the YouTube equivalent of an infomercial; that is, a video that shows the viewer how to do something useful, functioning as a teaser for the additional products and services you sell. For example, let's say you sell automobile parts. To promote your product, you create a short YouTube video about how to change your car's oil or how to adjust the engine's timing. At the beginning and end of the video you display a title card or graphic with your website address and maybe even your company's toll-free phone number. Because the video is rich in informational content (the how-to info), it attracts viewers—some of which will be interested enough to click through and purchase the parts you have for sale.

The key is to provide enough useful information to be of practical value to viewers, and then make it easy for those viewers to click through to your site for more information or to purchase what you have for sale. It can't be a straight advertisement; it has to be real information, presented in as direct a fashion as possible.

Educate and Sell

Another approach is to create a how-to video—that is, show the viewer how to do something useful. For example, if you sell appliance parts, you could create a video showing how to change the water filter in a refrigerator or the light bulb in a dryer. If you offer custom woodworking services, create a video showing how to build a bookcase or install wood trim. If you own a tire store, create a video showing how to check tire pressure or change a flat. You get the picture.

The key here is to offer truly useful content. Nothing theoretical or ethereal; down-to-earth practicality is what attracts YouTube viewers. Make the task common enough to draw a large audience, produce an easy to follow step-by-step tutorial, and then use the video to sell other goods and services.

Entertain and Sell

Informing and educating are important and will draw a fair number of YouTube viewers if you do it right. But everybody likes to be entertained, which is why pure entertainment videos typically show up at the top of YouTube's lists of most-viewed videos.

What's entertaining? Well, that depends on what you do and what you offer for sale. I like the example of Blendtec (www.youtube.com/user/Blendtec), a small company that sells high-end blenders. In a creative spurt, the company came up with a concept it calls "Will It Blend?" that it turned into a series of videos that spread across the Internet like wildfire. The videos, all extremely entertaining, showed the company's founder placing various objects—a video game cartridge, marbles, light bulbs, a can of soup, and so forth—into Blendtec blenders. A flip of the switch, and the viewer quickly discovered the answer to the question. The result was an Internet phenomenon as the videos turned viral—and all produced on a budget of less than $100.

note

Read a profile of Blendtec and its YouTube marketing immediately following Chapter 3, "Tips for Producing More Effective YouTube Videos."

Blendtec's example shows how a company can benefit from a creative idea, executed in an entertaining fashion. There is nothing particularly informative or educational about the "Will It Blend?" spots, but they are fun to watch. And as YouTube continues to prove, videos that are fun to watch get watched—a lot.

How Can You Use YouTube to Market Your Business?

Different companies have different goals for the online component of their marketing mix. Maybe they're trying to generate brand awareness. Maybe they're trying to promote a particular product or drive sales to their retail store or website. Whatever your goal, YouTube can and should be an important part of your overall marketing mix.

In addition, you can use YouTube for purposes other than sales. For example, you can incorporate YouTube as part of your product or customer support mix, use videos for product training, and even incorporate YouTube for recruiting and employee communications. Anything you can say in person or to a group of people, you can say in a video and distribute via YouTube.

YouTube for Brand Awareness

Large national companies and major advertisers often use YouTube to enhance the awareness of their brands. Instead of focusing on individual products or services, these videos push the company's brand, often in the same fashion used in traditional television advertising.

In fact, online videos are better at imparting brand awareness than are traditional TV ads. A Millward Brown study found that online viewing led to 82% brand awareness and 77% product recall, compared to just 54% brand awareness and 18% product recall for similar television ads. Experts believe this is because online viewers are more engaged than television viewers; the Web is a more interactive medium than the passive viewing inherent with television.

Brand awareness videos are typically entertaining, using a soft-sell approach to ingrain the brand's name and image in the minds of viewers. The Coca-Cola Company took this approach in 2006, creating a Holiday Wishcast mini-hub on the YouTube site. This hub employed the company's famous animated polar bears and other holiday branding, subtly pushing Coke as the drink of choice for the holiday season.

YouTube for Product Advertising

If you can use YouTube to push an overall brand, you can use it to push individual products, too. This requires a more direct approach, although it's still important to make the video informative, educational, or entertaining.

To promote a product, you want to show the product in your advertising, as Blendtec did with its blender videos and Nike did with its clips for Tiempo Ronaldinho shoes. You can show the product in action or used as part of a demonstration or tutorial. Just make sure you include lots of close-up product shots and link back to your own website—where more product information is available.

YouTube for Retail Promotion

You can also use YouTube to promote a company's retail stores. These videos can be general in nature (which gives the videos a long shelf life), or more specifically targeted to shorter-term promotions ("check out this weekend's specials!").

But a video that is nothing more than a store advertisement probably won't attract a lot of viewers. A better approach is to find a way to showcase the store without resorting to claims of 20% off and "this weekend only" specials. For example, you might want to record a short store tour or highlight individual departments or services within the store. Make the video informative, and you stand a better chance of grabbing eyeballs.

YouTube for Direct Sales

YouTube is a terrific channel for generating direct sales for products and services. All you have to do is show the product in action or provide a clip of the service in question, and then ask for the sale by directing the viewer to your website.

One of the best ways to showcase a product is in an instructional video—the online equivalent of an old-school infomercial. Do you remember Ron Popeil's late-night TV ads for slicers and dicers? Create a shorter version of said Ronco ads, but focusing on the useful attributes of your product, and you'll gain YouTube viewership.

The key to converting eyeballs to dollars is to generously highlight your company's website address or 800-number within the body of the video. Put the contact information at the front of the video, at the end of the video, and overlaid at the bottom of the screen during the body of the clip. Make it easy for interested viewers to find more information or place an order. (And, to that end, there's nothing wrong with mentioning the product's price somewhere in the video.)

YouTube for Product Support

Not all companies use YouTube to generate new business; some companies do so to support existing customers. Consider some of the most common customer problems and questions, and produce one or more videos
addressing those issues. If you can help your customers help themselves,
you provide them with a useful service and reduce your company's support costs—all with a free YouTube video.

Let's say that, for example, you sell do-it-yourself DVD racks—the kind
that have to be assembled. Let's also assume that some of your customers
have trouble putting the racks together, resulting in a flood of calls to
your customer support center. If you record a short video demonstrating
how to put one of your racks together and post that video to YouTube,
you can direct your customers to that video if they have problems. For
that matter, you can embed the YouTube video into your website, using
YouTube to host the video. It doesn't matter where customers view the
video, YouTube or your site; what matters is that they get their problems
solved at little or no expense to you.

note

Learn more about embedding YouTube videos on your company's site in
Chapter 11, "Incorporating YouTube Videos on Your Own Website."

The same goes if you have specific product support or technical support
issues. If you're a computer manufacturer, you might create a video showing users how to install more memory or connect an external hard drive.
If you're a car manufacturer, you might create a video showing drivers
how to change a brake light or check their car's oil level. You get the
idea—use YouTube to turn a problem area into a public relations victory.

YouTube for Product Training

Your company can also use YouTube for internal purposes. Take, for
example, the issue of product training. You have a new product to introduce and a sales force to train. How best to reach them? In the old days,
you'd fly salespeople from around the country to a central office and put
on a day's worth of hands-on training. Doing so, however, is both time-
consuming and expensive.

Instead, consider using YouTube for your product training. Create a series
of short training videos, upload them to YouTube, and provide access to
all your company's salespeople. Sales force personnel can watch the

videos at their leisure, without losing valuable sales time trekking back to the office for training. You save money, your salespeople save time, and you create an archive of product information that anyone can access at any time.

> **note**
>
> If you create a video for internal use, make it a private video so that it won't be viewable by the public. Learn how to do this in Chapter 9, "Uploading Your Videos to YouTube."

YouTube for Employee Communications

You can use YouTube for all manner of company communications. Instead of holding a big company meeting just so that the big boss can give his yearly state of the company address, have him record the address and post it on a private channel on YouTube. Employees can watch the prez say his thing from the comfort of their own desks, while they're on the road, or even at home.

In fact, many companies find that YouTube is a fast and effective way to disseminate all kinds of employee information. Done right, it gets information out there in near–real-time, with all the benefit of face-to-face communication, which is a lot better than sending impersonal memos via email.

YouTube for Recruiting

Finally, don't underestimate YouTube as a recruitment tool for new employees. If you have a company welcome video, post it on YouTube and make it public. Think of this as a PR exercise to attract new talent to your company, which means doing it up right—it's as much a marketing project as it is something from the HR department.

You can link to the video from all your recruiting materials, even from any traditional ads you place. Don't limit yourself to a single long puff video: Produce separate videos for individual departments, as well as to illustrate company values, employee benefits, facilities, and the like.

> **tip**
>
> Your current employees are your best recruitment tools. Include plenty of employee interviews in your recruitment videos to help personalize your company and to put a friendly face on the corporation.

The Big Picture

As you can see, there are lots of ways your company can make use of YouTube videos—from traditional brand and product marketing to customer support and employee communications. In almost all instances, you don't have to spend a fortune doing it; as you'll learn, you can produce YouTube videos in a quick and inexpensive fashion. And, of course, you don't have to give a penny to YouTube; everything you post on the YouTube site is completely free of charge.

The key is to not over think or over analyze the opportunity. Don't be afraid to get started, even if your first videos are modest with little budget behind them. YouTube makes it easy to dip your toes in the water; you can't reap the benefit until you get online! ■

2

Developing Your YouTube Marketing Strategy

Before you shoot your first minute of video footage, you need to determine how YouTube fits into your marketing plans. What is *your* YouTube marketing strategy—what do you want to achieve, and how?

Developing a YouTube marketing strategy is similar to developing any marketing strategy. You need to focus on your customer (audience), your message, your products/services/brand, and the other elements of your marketing mix. Everything has to work together to bring your chosen message to your chosen customer and generate the desired results.

You can't just shoot a video and throw it on the YouTube site; you need to develop a plan. This chapter walks you through the elements of a successful YouTube marketing strategy—what you need to do, why, and how.

What Is the Purpose of Your YouTube Videos?

Let's start with the most basic strategic issues for any marketing professional: What is the purpose of your YouTube videos? What is your goal? Why do you want to market via YouTube?

The wrong answer to the last question is "because everyone's doing it." Equally wrong are "because it's the latest thing," "because my competitors are doing it," and "because it's neat." As a marketing professional, you can't base your marketing strategy on the latest trends and technologies or on the behaviors of other marketers. You have to pick and choose the media you use based on their strategic importance to your company and brand; you have to pick media that serves your purpose and achieves your stated results.

It's possible that there is no strategic reason for you to market on YouTube. Perhaps you run a local contracting business and you have a loyal customer base, enough to fill your schedule for the next several months. In this instance, you might have nothing to gain by putting up a video on YouTube.

On the other hand, maybe you *do* have something to gain from producing a series of YouTube videos. Even if you don't want or need to attract new customers, you might be able to serve your existing customers better by incorporating YouTube into your media mix. Perhaps you can create a video demonstrating some of the options you have available for your customers, using YouTube as a kind of extended video catalog. Or maybe you can reinforce your new customers' choices by uploading testimonials from older customers. Possibly you can use YouTube as after-sale support by showing customers how to maintain the work you create for them.

The point is that you need to determine up front what you want to achieve, and how YouTube can help you achieve that. Don't automatically assume that YouTube is just for attracting new customers or selling individual products—there are a number of ways that you can use YouTube for both presale promotion and after-sale support. Figure out your goals ahead of time and then build your plan around those goals. And, as I said, if YouTube doesn't help you achieve those goals, that's okay; you should never shoehorn a particular medium into your plans, just because everybody else thinks you ought to.

Who Is Your Customer?

Another factor in determining how YouTube fits into your plans is the customers you're trying to reach. Just who do you sell to—and why?

This is Marketing 101 stuff, so forgive me if I'm stating the obvious. But many marketers, especially those working online, either don't know the basics or somehow forget them over time. Sometimes stating the obvious is the most important thing you can do.

All your marketing should revolve around the customer, so it's imperative that you know who that customer is and what he wants. Work through the following checklist to determine just who it is you should be focusing on:

- How old is your target customer?
- Is your customer male or female?
- Is your customer single or married?
- What is your customer's average yearly income?
- Where does your customer live?
- Where does your customer shop?
- What does your customer like to do in his or her spare time?
- How does your customer describe himself or herself?
- How does your customer prefer to receive information: via newspaper, television, radio, or the Internet?
- What websites does your customer frequent?
- What products does your customer currently use?
- Is your target customer a current client or someone who is not yet using your product?
- Does your customer know about your company or product?
- If so, what does your customer think about your company and product—what image does he have of you?

These are just a few of the things you need to know about your target customer. The more you know, of course, the better you can serve the customer's wants and needs. The less you know, the more you're guessing in the dark—and guessing in the dark is an ineffective and inefficient way to create a marketing plan.

Of course, another set of important questions to ask, in terms of incorporating YouTube into your marketing mix, concerns YouTube itself. Does your customer visit the YouTube site? If so, how often? Why does he visit the site? What does he think of YouTube? What types of videos does he like to watch? How does he feel about "commercial" videos on YouTube?

If your customer is a heavy YouTube viewer, and if he's open to commercial messages among his entertainment, YouTube holds promise as a marketing vehicle for your company. On the other hand, if your customer never visits YouTube, or is diametrically opposed to commercial messages intruding on his entertainment, you shouldn't include YouTube in your marketing mix. After all, you don't want to advertise in places where your customer isn't.

note

Who uses YouTube? A 2008 Bear Stearns research report notes that the 25–54 age group viewed 63% of YouTube videos; under-25s accounted for 27% of video viewing. Other researchers indicate that YouTube's gender ratio is approximately 60/40 male/female.

What Does Your Customer Want or Need?

Knowing who your customer is makes up just part of the process. Equally important is knowing what your customer wants or needs—that is, why the customer is in the market for a particular product or service.

Perhaps the customer has a problem; most do. Your customer is looking for a solution to that problem—and that solution is what you want to provide.

Or perhaps the customer has a basic unfulfilled need, such as food, shelter, or security. Your goal is to fulfill that basic need; the product or service you offer is how to fill the need.

What's key is to identity with your customer so that you share his wants and needs. Only then can you determine how to best meet those requirements and communicate that fact in a compelling fashion.

What Are You Promoting?

What exactly is it that you want to promote on YouTube? Is it your overall company, a brand, or an individual product or service? You need to identify this upfront because you'll use different methods to promote different aspects of your business.

And, remember, you're not always promoting a product. That is, your product might be only the means to an end. For example, you might be selling bookcases, but what you're actually promoting is a superior system for displaying your customers' libraries of books. Or maybe you're selling door locks; what you're promoting are the security and peace of mind that come from a superior lock solution.

In other words, you're promoting a solution, not a product or service. Your product or service is merely a means to accomplish that solution.

Or maybe you're not promoting anything at all. That is, you might be using YouTube in a support role to provide customer support or technical support; that's much different from using YouTube to sell products or services. It's also possible that you use YouTube for strictly internal purposes, to support your employee base or for employee training. Again, how you intend to use YouTube will determine the types of videos you create.

What Is Your Message?

Assuming that you use YouTube to promote your company, brand, or product/service, what message is it that you want to impart? Marketing is about more than just offering a product for sale; it's also about creating and conveying a company/brand/product image—and that image is conveyed as part of a cohesive marketing message.

Take, for example, the classic example of low-end versus high-end image. If you sell a commodity product on price, the image you convey must resonate with a price-sensitive audience. On the other hand, if you offer a high-end product to a brand-savvy audience, you need to convey a classier image; it's not about price, it's about appearance.

Beyond simple image, your YouTube videos need to carry the same or similar message that you use in your other advertising media. This message is critical to everything you do in your marketing efforts; it should grab your customers' attention, tell them how you can solve their problems/meet their needs, and convince them that you offer the best of all available solutions.

That last point bears reinforcement. Not only should you tell potential customers what it is you're offering, but you also must tell them what it is about your company/brand/product that differentiates you from your competitors. Answer the unspoken question, "why us?"—or you risk losing the sale to a better-defined competitor. Emphasize what makes you different and what makes you better. You are selling yourself, after all.

In doing this, however, you should never forget that your message is about the customer, not about you. The biggest mistake that companies make is to communicate "what we do" instead of "what we do for you." Customers want to hear what's in it for them, not what's in it for you.

In addition, you must present your message in terms of benefits rather than features. Never describe the 22 function buttons on your new electronic gizmo; instead, describe how each button solves a particular customer want/need. Instead of saying that your gizmo has memory recall, say that "memory recall lets you remember key contacts at the touch of a single button." Again, phrase your message in terms of what you do for the customer—not in terms of what you or your product does.

How Does YouTube Fit Within Your Overall Marketing Mix?

As I said at the outset of this chapter, this is all Marketing 101 stuff—customer, message, and so on. What's different, in the YouTube age, is that you have this new medium in which to reach the customer and impart your message. How, then, should YouTube fit within the rest of your marketing mix?

A company's marketing mix today looks a whole lot different from the marketing mix of a generation ago. Go back a decade or two and you had a limited number of media to use: newspapers, magazines, radio, television, and direct mail. All those media are still around, and still important, but now you have a new family of media built around that channel that we call the Internet.

What new media am I talking about? Here's a short list:

- Email
- Websites
- Search engines
- Blogs
- Social networks (such as Facebook and MySpace)
- Photo-sharing sites (Flickr and so on)
- Video-sharing sites (YouTube and its competitors)

This book isn't about all those other Internet-related media, just YouTube. Still, you need to consider all aspects of online marketing when fitting YouTube into your marketing plans. Does your YouTube marketing stand alone, or is it part of a larger campaign that includes seeded blog postings, banner website ads, pay-per-click search engine ads, targeted emails, and viral campaigns on the key social networks? This should all be determined up front.

In addition, YouTube's place alongside the traditional marketing media should also be determined. Do you use YouTube merely as another channel for your television commercials, or does it expand on your television advertising with additional spots, alternative takes, expanded scenarios, and the like? Does YouTube merely provide more exposure for your exist-ing campaign, or does it change things up to fine-tune your message to the slightly younger, more interactive YouTube audience?

For example, let's say you have an established campaign that uses the traditional media of print and television. The easiest approach is simply to repurpose your television ads to YouTube, posting your 30-second TV commercials to the YouTube site.

This is a simple approach, and it might be a good one—if your commer-cials are compelling enough to attract YouTube viewers. But, let's face it, when given the choice of watching a million other entertaining and informative videos, why would YouTube viewers choose to spend 30 sec-onds of their valuable time to watch the same commercial they've seen a dozen times on TV? Again, if the commercial is compelling enough, this might work. But for most advertisers that approach, although inexpensive and easy to execute, won't be successful.

A better approach might be to take your existing television commercial and expand it for the YouTube audience. Maybe offer an "uncut" or "uncensored" version or shoot a new commercial that starts up where the first one left off. Or maybe use YouTube as a channel for similar execu-tions that you didn't use on television. Something to extend or expand your existing campaign, not just replicate it online.

You can also use your existing campaign as the jumping off point for something new and creative. For example, some companies have created an initial video and then encouraged viewers to produce their own varia-tions. You can even do it in the form of a contest: Make your own YouTube video promoting our product, and the winner gets a valuable prize. Use your imagination and take advantage of the user interaction that YouTube encourages.

Finally, you can move beyond your existing campaign and create some-thing totally new for YouTube. Play to the differences inherent in the YouTube medium; create a video campaign that exploits what's new and unique about YouTube. Just make sure your YouTube-specific activity hews to the same overall message you use in the rest of your marketing.

Whichever approach you adopt, make the choice based on your particu-lar circumstances. You can repurpose your existing marketing materials for YouTube; you can extend them with the YouTube medium and audi-ence in mind; or you can create something completely new for the YouTube channel. There's no one right way to proceed. In fact, you might choose different approaches for different campaigns over time.

How Will You Measure the Results of Your YouTube Videos?

Creating a video and posting it on YouTube is just part of the process. How do you measure the success of that video?

The first key to measuring success is to determine what kind of response you wanted. Did you design the video to generate direct sales, either via your website or 800-number? Did you design the video to drive traffic to your website? Did you design the video to enhance or reinforce your company or brand image? Or did you design the video to reduce customer or technical support costs?

This is key: To measure the success of your YouTube video, you have to first determine what it is you hope to achieve. Then, and only then, can you measure the results:

- If your goal is to generate sales, measure sales. Include your website's URL and 800-number in the video, along with a promotion or order code, and then track sales that include that code.

- If your goal is to drive traffic to your website, measure your traffic pre- and post-YouTube video. Use site analytics to determine where site traffic originates from; specifically track the traffic that came directly from the YouTube site.

- If your goal is to build your brand image, measurement is more difficult. You need to conduct some sort of market research after your YouTube campaign has had a chance to do its thing and ask customers what they think of your brand—and where they heard about it.

- If your goal is to reduce customer or technical support costs, measure the number of support requests before and after uploading the YouTube video. The more effective the video, the fewer the subsequent calls for support.

Of course, another way to measure your video's success is to count the number of views it achieves on YouTube. This, however, is a false measurement. Just because many people view your video doesn't mean that it has accomplished the goals you set out to achieve. A video with 100,000 views is nice, but it means nothing if you wanted to boost your sales and it didn't do that. Entertaining YouTube viewers is one thing but generating sales (or establishing brand image or whatever) is quite another.

What Type of Video Content Is Best for Your Goals?

What type of video should you produce for YouTube? More immediately, what type of video *can* you produce?

You have a number of choices to make when determining what type of videos to produce for you YouTube. It's not a one-size-fits-all situation; what works for one company might bomb completely for another. In fact, what works today might not be what you need to do tomorrow. And, of course, you're not limited to a single approach; many companies employ two or more different types of videos, each designed to achieve its own specific goal.

With that in mind, let's look at the most common types of videos that companies incorporate into their online marketing mixes.

Repurposed Commercials

Many companies think that the best way to use YouTube is as an alternative distribution channel for their existing television commercials. Their YouTube content consists of repurposed commercials—the same 30-second spots they run on television.

This might be an appropriate strategy—if your TV spots are uniquely entertaining. To be honest, however, this is a losing strategy for most firms; YouTube viewers tend to expect something new and different than the same commercials they see on TV.

In fact, some companies have experienced the ire of the YouTube community for unimaginatively commercializing the site in this manner. You win the support of the community by doing something new and innovative; you lose their support when you seemingly don't put in the effort or treat YouTube as just another type of television station—which it most decidedly is not.

---

tip

In my opinion, YouTube is not the place to recycle your company's commercials. Users will not go out of the way to view something online that they try to avoid otherwise in the real world. Unless you have a clever, Super Bowl–worthy commercial that people want to view again and again, keep your ads to yourself and don't upload them to YouTube.

That said, if you have no budget for new production and you do have a unique commercial message, you might want to try uploading your existing commercials to the YouTube site. Know, however, that what works on the big TV screen often works less well in the small YouTube video window.

For example, it's important to note that most YouTubers view videos in a 320×240 pixel window. That's pretty small when compared to the 640×480 resolution of a 25" standard definition television screen, or the 1920×1080 resolution of a 42" or larger high definition TV. All the niggling details you can see on a bigger TV turn miniscule when viewed in a web browser. This fact alone might cause you to reshoot a busy television commercial for the smaller YouTube screen; at the very least, you want to decrease the resolution before uploading the video.

---

note

Learn more about optimizing your videos for the YouTube audience in Chapter 4, "Understanding Audio/Video Technology."

Infomercials

Let's move beyond repurposed material into new content created expressly for the YouTube site. (Although you can, of course, also display your YouTube videos on your own website or blog.) When you create videos just for YouTube, you can choose from among several different approaches you can employ.

One popular approach is to create the YouTube equivalent of an infomercial. That is, you create a video that purports to convey some type of information but, in reality, exists to subtly plug your product or brand.

Let's say that you offer gift baskets for sale. You create a short video for YouTube about how to make gift baskets—something that would be of interest to anyone in the market for them. You prominently display your web page address and phone number within the video and in the descriptive text that accompanies the video on the YouTube site. Because the video has some informational content (the how-to information), it attracts viewers, and a certain percentage of them will follow through to purchase the gift baskets you have for sale.

Or maybe you're a business consultant and you want to promote your consulting services. To demonstrate what you have to offer potential clients, you create and upload some sort of short video—a motivational lecture, perhaps, or a slideshow about specific business practices, or something similar. You use the video to establish your expert status and then display your email address or web page address to solicit business for your consulting services.

Or maybe you have a full-length DVD for sale. You excerpt a portion of the DVD and upload it to YouTube, with graphics before and after (and maybe even during) the video detailing how the full-length DVD can be ordered.

Likewise if you're a musician with CDs to sell, an author with books to sell, an artist with paintings or other artwork to sell, or a craftsman with various crafts and such to sell. The musician might create a music video to promote his CDs; the author might read an excerpt from her book; the artist might produce a photo slideshow of her work; and the craftsman might upload a short video walk-through of pieces he has for sale. Make sure you include details for how the additional product can be ordered and let your placement on YouTube do the promotion for you.

Here's an example of an effective infomercial approach. Viator Travel (www.youtube.com/user/ViatorTravel) offers tours of more than 400 destinations worldwide. The company created a series of informative and entertaining videos about its top destinations and uploaded those videos to YouTube. Interested people can view the videos and then contact the firm to schedule a vacation. It's quite synergistic.

Then there's John Pullum (www.youtube.com/user/Hypnotions), a hypnotist and mind reader who provides corporate entertainment and motivational speeches. He's uploaded videos of several of his appearances to YouTube; they're both entertaining and informational in regard to the services that he has to offer. Any viewers who like what they see can then go to his website to learn more or arrange an engagement.

The key is to create a video that people actually want to watch. That means something informative, useful, or entertaining. It can't be a straight commercial because people don't like to watch commercials. It has to provide value to the viewer.

After you hook the viewers, you lead them back to your website where your goods or services are for sale. It's a two-step process: Watch the video and then go to the website to learn more or buy something. If your video is interesting enough, viewers will make the trip to your website to close the deal.

Instructional Videos

Similar to the infomercial is the instructional or how-to video. In this type of video, you create something truly useful for your target customer and then drive business by direct link from the instructional video.

Let's say, for example, that you sell appliance parts. You create a series of videos showing, in step-by-step fashion, how to perform various types of repairs: changing the drive belt in a dryer, cleaning the burner assemblies in a gas range, and so on. Each video exists unto itself, with the sole goal of providing practical information to the viewer. Of course, you include your website address and 800-number at the start and end of each video and suggest that viewers can find additional information (and the parts they need) on your website. You help the viewers and they (eventually) buy something from you.

Product Presentations and Demonstrations

You can also use YouTube for more obvious selling efforts, the most common of which is the product presentation or demonstration. Here is where you use the video medium to show customers a particular product, in the kind of detail you just can't do in print or on a web page.

Many products are good candidates for video demonstrations—especially mobile phones, MP3 players, digital cameras, and other difficult-to-use electronic gadgets. Automobiles also benefit from video presentation because there's a lot to see there. In fact, any item that's not quickly or easily understood, or that has a bevy of sophisticated features, is a good candidate for a YouTube video demonstration.

Real Estate Walk-Throughs

A specific subset of the product demonstration is the real estate walk-through video. Today, most realtors take digital photographs of the houses they list, and potential buyers view those photos on the realtor's website. But there's nothing stopping you from using a camcorder to produce a video tour of the house, editing the tour into a short video, and posting the video on YouTube. You can then direct potential buyers to the walk-through video on the YouTube website or embed the YouTube video on your website so that visitors can view the video there. It's a great enhancement to a realtor's selling services, and it doesn't cost you a dime (beyond the cost of shooting the video, of course).

Customer Testimonials

You can also use YouTube to promote your company or reinforce a buyer's decision. To that end, the time-honored approach of using testimonials from existing customers is a viable one. Send a video crew out to the customer's location, or invite him or her to your office, and let the camera roll. Film the customer talking about her experience with your company in her own words, and you have an effective plug for who you are and what you do.

Company Introductions

For that matter, you can use YouTube to introduce your company to your customers. This could be in the form of a short brand-building video or a video welcome from the company president—even a video tour of your offices or factory. This is especially beneficial for companies that employ innovative production techniques or create especially interesting products.

Expert Presentations

If your business is a leader in its category, or if you are an industry expert, you can establish and exploit that expertise via a series of YouTube videos. All it takes is a video camera or webcam pointed at you behind a desk; you then spend three or four minutes talking about a particular topic or issue of interest. If you truly know what you're talking about, your video can help to establish your professional credentials and burnish your company's image.

Business Video Blogs

This leads us to the topic of video blogs, or *vlogs*. A vlog is like a normal text-based blog, except that it's spoken and put on video. You or someone from your company sits in front of a webcam or video camera and expounds on the issues of the day. Perhaps multiple vloggers participate so that you present a variety of faces to the viewing public. In any case, you use the video blog as you would a normal blog: to comment on contemporary issues and put a human face on your company.

Executive Speeches

If your company likes to communicate regularly to its employees, YouTube presents a better way to do so. Instead of sending a soulless memo to the worker bees or trying to gather all your employees at a single location, simply record your company executives on video and post those videos on YouTube. Create a private channel just for your company's employees, and they can receive the executive's message at any time, on their own computers. It's more efficient than a company meeting and more personal than a memo.

Company Seminars and Presentations

Along the same line, you can use YouTube to bring all your company's employees into seminars and presentations that might otherwise be limited to a select few. You might accomplish this by recording a meeting or seminar with one or more video cameras, or by uploading PowerPoint presentations in a video format with audio annotations. Again, this works best via a private company channel that authorized employees can view at their discretion.

tip

To convert PowerPoint presentations to video with audio accompaniment, use a software program called Camtasia (www.techsmith.com).

User or Employee Submissions

Of course, you don't have to personally create all the videos you post to YouTube. There's a wealth of talent outside your company's marketing department, in the form of other employees, customers, and just interested individuals.

You might, for example, solicit videos from your company's employee base. Run a contest, pay for participation, or just present the endeavor as a fun exercise, but let your coworkers express their creativity in ways that are hopefully suitable for YouTube broadcast.

The same goes with your customers, who have their own ways of showing brand or company loyalty. Ask for testimonials, as discussed previously, or open it up to more fully produced submissions. As with employee videos, you can roll the whole thing up into a contest, which serves as another form of promotion for your company.

Humorous Spots

Finally, don't fall into the trap of taking yourself too seriously. Some of the most popular videos on YouTube are humorous ones; the funnier the video, the likely it is to gain a large audience and go viral. It's okay to make fun of your company, your product, or yourself, or just to treat the topic in an entertaining fashion. YouTubers like to be entertained, and they'll tolerate a promotional message if it's a funny one.

The Big Picture

As you can see, a lot of thought goes into creating a successful YouTube video. It's not just a matter of recycling an existing spot, or even of setting up a camera and pressing the Record button. You need to determine what you want the YouTube video to achieve, who your audience is, how your video fits within your overall marketing mix, and how you intend to measure the results. Then, and only then, can you decide what type of video to produce—and then start working on it.

When marketing on YouTube, as with marketing in any medium, planning is everything. ■

3

Tips for Producing More Effective YouTube Videos

So, you've decided to make YouTube part of your company's marketing mix and you've even decided what type of video to produce. How do you go about making a must-see video, one that draws viewers and generates sales for your business?

There's no one-size-fits-all approach to producing effective YouTube videos, but I can impart lots of tips that can guide you in the right direction. Read on to learn how to make better-looking, better-performing YouTube videos—and drive customers to your accompanying website.

Tips for Creating Better-Looking Videos

When shooting a video for YouTube, it's important to get the file format and technical details right. It's also important to get the visual details right—to create a video that is visually and stylistically interesting to YouTube viewers.

What works well on a big movie screen works less well on a smaller home television screen. Similarly, what looks good on a TV-sized screen doesn't look nearly as good when viewed in a small window in a web browser. If you want to create an effective YouTube video, you have to produce for the medium, exploiting those elements that make YouTube unique.

Get the Size Right

YouTube's default video size is 320 pixels wide by 240 pixels tall; some videos are available in the slightly larger 480-pixel×360-pixel size. In both cases, that's a small window—but one you have to produce for.

> **note**
>
> A *pixel* is the smallest element of a digital image, used to measure image resolu-
> tion. A standard definition television picture is 640 pixels wide by 480 pixels tall;
> a high-definition picture is, at minimum, 1280 pixels wide by 720 pixels tall.

Given the growing prevalence of 480×360 videos, you want to convert your videos to no smaller than this size; a 360×240 video looks blocky and grainy when blown up to 480×360. In fact, I recommend you shoot and upload your videos at 640×480 resolution. This is the same resolution as standard definition television and provides extra bandwidth in the event YouTube increases the size of its viewing window in the future.

So, shoot at 640×480 with a standard 4:3 aspect ratio. Don't shoot in widescreen because that merely leaves letterbox bars above and below your video—which is wasted space on the YouTube page. Also, don't bother shooting in high definition (1280×720 or 1920×1080) because, again, the extra resolution is lost to YouTube viewers.

> **tip**
>
> If your video will be used in other media besides YouTube and the Web, you may
> want to shoot at higher resolution—and then downconvert the video to better
> meet YouTube's specs.

Shoot for the Smaller Screen

Given that viewers will view your video in a small window in their web browser, you must create a video that looks good at this small size, viewed on a typical computer screen. What does this mean in terms of visual style?

Big and bright is the order of the day. You can shoot an epic with a cast of thousands, but those thousands will look like little dots in a small browser window. The best YouTube videos are visually simple, with a single main subject filling up most of the small video window. Get up close and frame the subject so that he or it fills most of the screen.

When using a webcam, filling the screen means getting up close to the lens. When using a camcorder, you should zoom into the main subject and remove any unnecessary people or objects from the frame. Close-ups are good; crowd shots aren't.

You also want to make sure the scene you shoot has adequate lighting. Too many YouTube videos come out way too dark, which makes them hard to view. This is especially important when you shoot with a webcam; even though a webcam might claim to work under normal room light, you're better off investing in a set of affordable photo floodlights or a separate speed light.

Finally, know that streaming video doesn't always reproduce rapid movement well. Move the camera too fast, or have your subject move too fast in the frame, and viewers are likely to see motion smears, pixilation, and other unacceptable video effects. Keep things slow and simple for best results.

Accentuate the Contrast

As noted previously, visual contrast is highly desirable with small-footprint videos. Put a pale or white-clad subject in front of a black background, or a black-clad subject in front of a white one. And consider using brightly colored backgrounds, which pop in YouTube thumbnails. Believe it or not, hot pink really grabs the attention of casual viewers!

caution

Contrast is good, but too much contrast can play nasty tricks with many webcams and camcorders. A bright white background can cause many cameras to darken the foreground subject, either reducing detail or casting the subject entirely into darkness. For this reason, always test your shooting environment before finalizing your video—including watching a test video on your computer screen.

Invest in Quality Equipment

To make a quality video, you need a quality video camera. That doesn't necessarily mean a professional camera; a high-quality, consumer-grade camcorder will do a good job. Make sure you have a digital camcorder, rather than an older analog one so that your video is completely digital from start to finish. Look for a camcorder that works good under low-light conditions, that has an attachment for external light, and that lets you connect an external microphone. Personally, I prefer hard disk camcorders because they make it easy to transfer video from the camcorder to your computer for editing; it's a simple matter of transferring files from one hard disk to another, without having to play back a tape in real time. And the bigger the camera's charge-coupled device (*CCD*), the better the picture quality.

---

note

Speaking of editing, you also need to invest in a fast computer and quality video-editing software. Learn more in Chapter 8, "Editing and Enhancing Your Video."

Shoot Professionally

When you shoot your video, embrace professional production techniques—even if you just use a consumer-grade camcorder. Here are the things you need to keep in mind:

- Make sure the subject is well lit; use an external lighting kit.
- Make sure the speaker can be heard; use an external microphone, if your camera has an auxiliary mic input.
- Monitor the audio with a set of headphones while rehearsing and recording; don't assume the camcorder is recording good sound just because the level meters are bouncing.
- Minimize background and crowd noise; keep it quiet on the set.
- Keep the camera steady; use a tripod.
- Don't move the camera around too much.
- Don't zoom in and out too much.

In other words, do everything you can to keep the focus on the main subject. Don't let the camerawork distract the viewer!

Use Two Cameras

Here's another way to add a professional sheen to your videos. Instead of shooting with a single camera directly in front of the subject, shoot with two cameras, shooting the subject from two different angles. This allows you to cut between shots in the editing process, adding visual variety to the video.

In addition, having two different angles to choose from makes it easier to edit the speaker, if you need to. Editing in different shots from different angles makes the fact that you're editing less apparent; the cut isn't as jarring or noticeable when you switch from one angle to another.

Be Professional—Or Not

If you're representing a professional business, your videos need to look professional. The standard look of personal YouTube videos—an unshaven twenty-something in a t-shirt, staring intently at a web camera—just doesn't give off the professional vibe that most businesses want. Whether your video's cast is one or thousands, make sure that anyone on camera is well dressed and well groomed, that everyone is well lit and well mic'd, and that the whole production has a professional sheen.

Unless, that is, you want to give out a hip young vibe. In that instance, take off the suits and ties and emulate the personal look that's become ubiquitous on YouTube. In other words, make sure your video has a look and feel that matches your company's message.

Don't Just Recycle Old Videos—Re-Edit Them, Too

Many businesses get started on YouTube by uploading existing company videos. This isn't a horrible idea, especially as a first effort. It's a low-cost, low-effort way to get your feet wet in the YouTube pond. However, your results will suffer if you just upload old videos without changes. You'll do better if you bring an older video up-to-date in its content and appearance, even if that means re-editing the video or shooting new scenes.

Consider Creating a Slideshow

If you don't need full-motion video or don't have access to a video camera, consider putting together a slideshow of still photographs. Just compile the photos into a slideshow, add background music or a voiceover, and upload the whole thing to YouTube. Likewise, some topics benefit from PowerPoint presentations, which you can also convert to video for uploading to YouTube.

Hire a Pro

Don't have the skills or equipment to create a video in-house? Hire an outside firm to produce the video for you. Every town has one or more video production companies that do this sort of thing. There's no need to reinvent the wheel; let the pros teach you the right way to do things.

tip

If your budget is tight, consider contacting the film or marketing department of a local college to recruit lower-cost student talent.

Break the Rules

Don't confuse these tips for creating better-looking videos with hard and fast rules. It's okay to think outside the box and do things a little different. For example, if you want to create a hip-looking video for a younger audience, it's permissible to take the camera off the tripod and go for a "shaky-cam" effect. Do whatever it takes to achieve the effect you want.

Tips for Improving Your Video Content

Even the best-looking video will fail miserably if the content isn't compelling—and compelling content can compensate for poor production values. Remember that what you shoot is more important than how you shoot it; it's the content, stupid!

When creating content for YouTube, you want to give viewers a reason to come back for future viewings and to share your video with others. It's this sharing that makes for a viral video—compelling content begs to be more widely viewed.

Be Entertaining

The first rule of YouTube content is the most obvious: Your video must be entertaining. Produce a boring video, and no one will watch it. People like to be entertained. Give the people what they want.

It doesn't matter what product you sell or what your message is. Find a way to make your product, service, brand, or company entertaining. Not necessarily funny (although that helps—as you'll learn shortly), but entertaining—at least enough to keep viewers watching for the entire length of the video.

note

Trust me on this one. There is absolutely no way on this planet to make a recycled corporate PowerPoint presentation entertaining.

Be Informative

Being entertaining is essential, but so is being informative. A good video needs some meat to it; ask yourself, "Where's the beef?"

The typical name for this combination of education and entertainment is *edutainment*. That is, useful information presented in an entertaining manner. People might come for the entertainment, but they stay for the information.

Go for the Funny

Remember when I said that your video needs to be entertaining? Well, in many instances, the best way to be entertaining is to be funny. People like to laugh—and they remember the funny videos they view on YouTube.

It's a fact; the majority of top-rated videos on YouTube are funny ones. It's easier for a humorous video to go viral than it is for a deadly serious one to get the same exposure.

That means, of course, that you can't take yourself, your product, or your company too seriously. Your company needs a sense of humor and has to be able to laugh at itself. When you laugh at yourself, your audience will laugh with you, which establishes an emotional connection with your customer.

Keep It Short

One way to kill your video's entertainment value is to make it too long. Viewers today, and especially online, have a short attention span. The YouTube audience is the post-MTV generation, which means even a three-minute video has trouble holding its attention.

It's imperative, then, that you keep your videos short enough so that viewers don't tune out midway through. How short is short? It depends on who you ask; some experts say five minutes at the top end, some say one minute or less, and some even say 20 seconds is ideal. My recommendation is to keep your video no longer than two or three minutes—and the shorter, the better. Videos longer than three minutes or so typically don't get big viewership.

That doesn't mean you have to produce a video that's exactly three minutes long. As I said, shorter is better. If you can say what you want to say in 60 seconds, great. If you need the full three minutes, take it. But take into account viewers' short attention spans, and present your message quickly and efficiently.

tip

If you have a message that takes more than three minutes to present, consider chopping it up into multiple shorter videos that you can then combine into a YouTube playlist. For example, if you want to post a ten-minute speech, edit it into four segments of two to three minutes apiece.

Keep It Simple

You don't have to spend a lot of money on a YouTube video for it to be effective. In fact, it's easy for a company to spend too much money on its videos; the result is typically an overproduced monstrosity that looks horrible online. In many cases, a single person talking directly to a camera is all you need.

Stay Focused

Part of keeping it simple is focusing on a single message. Remember, you have only a few minutes at most to communicate to YouTube viewers. Don't spend that time trying to show your entire product line, or even multiple features of a sophisticated product. Hone in on a single product and communicate its strongest feature or benefit. One video per product or feature should be your rule.

Communicate a Clear Message

Whether you produce a talking-head video or one with a cast of thousands, make sure the message of your video is clear. Viewers have to come away with a clear idea of what you're selling and why they need it. Don't let the production get in the way of the message.

One way to do this is to test your video by showing it to a few people—family, friends, colleagues, whatever. Ask them to give you a single-sentence description of what they've just seen. If they can't repeat your message simply and succinctly, then you haven't communicated your message well—and you have more work to do.

Avoid the Hard Sell

Even though your message should be clear, you don't have to hit the viewers over the head with it. On YouTube, the soft sell works better than the hard sell. That's why a how-to video showing your product in use typically works better than a straight-ahead product demonstration; the former is a soft sell that communicates a subtle message to the viewers—who will typically turn off a harder message.

In other words, infomercials and edutainment are better than straight advertisements. In fact, if a video feels like an ad, most YouTube viewers will avoid it like the plague.

---

tip

If you show your product in a video, make sure you show it well. You need to clearly demonstrate your product throughout the course of the video; fortunately, video is uniquely suited for this sort of detailed product demonstration.

Keep It Fresh

The video you create today will be forgotten a month or two from now. With users posting thousands of new videos on YouTube every day, your video will quickly become yesterday's news. This requires you to update your company's video library continually; you need to either replace or refresh older videos on a regular basis. If you go more than a few months without posting a new video, your company's channel will lose viewership.

Design for Remixing

Here's a tip for advanced video marketers. The Internet and YouTube encourage interactivity; passive viewership is rapidly becoming a thing of the past. To that end, consider the act of remixing when creating your videos. That is, design a video that viewers can edit, adding their own dialog and music, or even cutting and pasting elements in a different order. When you encourage viewer interaction, you make a stronger connection with potential customers; you make them feel as if they're part of the process, and thus uniquely invested in your success.

Tips for Generating Sales

Creating a highly viewed video is great, but it's ultimately meaningless unless you can convert those viewers into paying customers. How, then, do you turn views into sales? Here are a few tips that can help in the process.

Include Your Website's Address in the Video

The key to marketing on YouTube is to lead viewers from your video on the YouTube site to your company's website—where you can then directly sell your products and services. How can you accomplish that?

Unfortunately, YouTube doesn't allow live links from a video to a third-party website. You can, however, include your website address in the body of the video and hope that viewers will remember it or write it down for future reference.

There's no point being subtle about this. Because people have trouble remembering things such as 800-numbers and URLs (*uniform resource locators*, also known as website addresses), you need to include your address early and often in the video. I recommend starting your video with a blank title screen with the URL overlaid, as shown in Figure 3.1. You should also end the video with a similar blank screen with the URL displayed. Make sure the URL is big and easily readable; high contrast colors, such as white text on a black background (or vice versa), provide the best results.

FIGURE 3.1

A title screen with the company's URL prominently displayed.

note

Naturally, if your business is telephone-based instead of Internet-based, you can substitute your 800-number for the website address—or list them both, if you prefer.

You might even want to include your URL onscreen during the main part of your video. Use your video-editing program to overlay the URL, as shown in Figure 3.2. The URL shouldn't interfere with the main content, of course, but you should be able to overlay them in a nonintrusive way.

FIGURE 3.2

A URL superimposed on the bottom of the video screen.

---

note

How do you create title screens and overlay text on a video? By using a video-editing program, as discussed in Chapter 8.

Include Your URL in the Accompanying Text

You can't live link from within a YouTube video; unfortunately, you also can't include a link to your website in the description that accompanies the video. You can, however, include your URL in the text description, but not as a live link. So, when you write the description for your video, make sure you include your URL or 800-number in the text.

Link from Your Profile

Although you can't include a live link in your video or its accompanying text, you can include a direct link to your website in your YouTube profile. Anyone clicking your username sees your profile with the link to your website, as shown in Figure 3.3. When viewers click the website link, they're taken directly to your site—where you can sell them more of what you have to offer.

FIGURE 3.3

A typical YouTube profile, complete with a live link to an accompanying website.

The Big Picture

What's the takeaway from all the tips presented in this chapter? The big picture is that you need to create professional-looking videos that are both entertaining and informative, and then make it easy for viewers to go to your website for more information or to purchase what you have to sell. Your videos can be funny or educational (or both), but they most definitely should be short; YouTubers have a notoriously short attention span. And, whatever type of video you produce, you should design it to be visually appealing in the small YouTube video window. There's no point including a cast of thousands when everyone has to fit in a space only a few inches across! ■

YouTube BUSINESS PROFILE

Profile: Blendtec

Imagine a staid, little blender company attaining cult status because of its YouTube videos. It happened—and the company is reaping the financial rewards.

Company Profile

Company: Blendtec

Product: Blenders

YouTube channel: www.youtube.com/user/Blendtec

Websites: www.blendtec.com, www.willitblend.com

Inside Blendtec

The company behind the cult video campaign is Blendtec, a division of a company called K-TEC. The parent company has been around since 1975, when company founder Tom Dickson created the K-TEC Kitchen Mill, an innovative way to mill wheat into flour. The company adopted the Blendtec name in 1999, when Dickson jumped on the smoothie revolution by creating durable, high-performance blenders for commercial use. Some of Blendtec's revolutions included electronic controls, programmable blend cycles, and other innovations for the company's commercial customers.

Today, Blendtec commercial blenders, dispensers, and mixers are found in restaurants, juice bars, ice cream parlors, and similar establishments around the world. The company has branched out to create consumer versions of its best-selling commercial products for use by trend-setting homemakers. These consumer products include the Mix n' Blend mixer/blender combo, the Total Blender tabletop blender, and the Connoisseur, the first in-counter blender designed for home use. Although the bulk of Blendtec's sales continue to be business-to-business, the new consumer line has become an ever-increasing part of the company's mix, with the typical customer being a female, aged 30–60.

The "Will It Blend?" Campaign

The company's growing consumer focus inspired its foray into YouTube marketing. Blendtec got the idea for its videos from actual destructive testing that had been going on at the company for years. Marketing Director George Wright happened upon owner Tom Dickson feeding a 2"×2" wooden board into a commercial blender as part of a destructive test and found it fascinating. He thought that others might get a kick out of watching the process, and the idea of creating a video was born.

The result was the production and release of the first five "Will It Blend?" videos. In these videos, Tom Dickson fed various items into Blendtec blenders to see whether they would actually blend. The items featured in these first videos included marbles, a rake handle, ice (blending into snow), a McDonald's Big Mac Extra Value Meal, and CoChicken (half Coke and half chicken). They all blended.

The videos proved quite YouTube-worthy. The response was immediate. Within the first week of posting, the company's videos had six million views. That's a true viral video!

The key to the "Will It Blend?" videos is that they're entertaining; it also helps that Dickson is a personable and completely engaged host. Will the Blendtec blender actually handle the item fed into it? What will the results look like? Will the results surprise Tom? What will he choose to blend next?

One of Blendtec's popular "Will It Blend?" videos.

Today, the company produces two types of "Will It Blend?" videos: Try This at Home and Don't Try This at Home. The latter category is by far the most popular because it features some ridiculous things to blend. (My favorite is the Chuck Norris video in which Tom Dickson blends a variety of action figures—with the Chuck Norris figure proving victorious.) As of May 2008, Blendtec has 64 videos online, and they're attracting 200 million views a month.

Low Costs, Big Results

Blendtec's "Will It Blend?" videos are amazingly cost-effective. Each video costs less than $20 to produce, using a typical consumer camcorder and existing locations in and around the company's office. There's nothing overly fancy here.

George Wright remarks, "We try to capture the sheer surprise of the blend...no preconceived notions, loose script, etc. For the most part, we will not even show Tom what we are blending until we are set up and ready to roll film."

So, that's how they get that spontaneous look and feel!

The sales of the Total Blender machine featured in the videos are a direct measurement of the effectiveness of the "Will It Blend?" campaign. Since the advent of the campaign, Total Blender sales have increased 500%. Incredible!

Advice for Other Businesses

Blendtec sticks with what works. The most recent of its 64 videos looks quite similar to the company's original videos; each video is short and sweet. What has changed is the fan response—several of the subjects have been suggested by the company's fans. (And, yes, the company's videos have a huge fan base—including the band Weezer, who featured Blendtec's Tom Dickson in the video for its song "Pork and Beans.")

Wright believes that YouTube is critical to the company's ongoing success, and a crucial part of its marketing mix. The company has also expanded the "Will It Blend?" concept into the Will It Blog? blog, t-shirts, DVDs, live performances at trade shows, and its own website where it offers all the videos for online viewing and its line of blenders for purchase.

Blendtec's freestanding "Will It Blend?" website.

Going forward, the company has some new products in the pipeline that should help it build on the "Will It Blend?" concept. As George Wright notes, "'Will It Blend?' has been a great launch pad for us to become a recognized brand. We will continue to leverage this brand for new products."

And it all started with five simple YouTube videos.... ■

II

Producing Your YouTube Videos

4

Understanding Audio/Video Technology

Producing professional videos for YouTube requires an understanding of the audio and video technology that YouTube uses. The more you know about the technology, the more appropriate and better-looking videos you can create.

It's important to understand not just the technology used by YouTube, but also other audio/video production technologies. For example, what video file format do you want to use when shooting your videos? What file format is best for editing? Which file formats does YouTube support for uploading? Read on to get smarter about all this.

Understanding Compression

Key to all video file formats is the concept of file compression. That's because raw, uncompressed video files are extremely large; video information is quite complex and requires much storage space. Rather than force users to work with unmanageably large files, the video industry adopted the concept of file compression, which works to reduce the size of the video files.

Each different method of compression is a codec, short for compression/decompression. A *codec* is a system for compressing a large amount of video data into a smaller, more manageable file. The more efficient the codec, the smaller the resulting files.

It isn't all about size, however. Some codecs do a better job of maintaining video quality than do others. That is, some compression schemes create videos that are noticeably inferior to the original; other compression schemes create videos that look almost identical to the source material. *Lossy* codecs result in a loss of data and degradation in audio and video quality, whereas *lossless* codecs reproduce the source material with no loss in quality.

Not only are different codecs better or worse at reproducing the source material, often you also have the option of selecting different degrees of compression within a codec. That is, you can encode the video data at different rates (measured in kilobytes per second, or *Kbps*). The higher the encoding rate, the better the resulting quality—and the larger the resulting file. For example, a file encoded at 256Kbps would theoretically have twice the resolution or quality as a file encoded at 128Kbps. Which file format and codec you choose represents a compromise between file size and audio/video quality—with the issue of compatibility thrown in for good measure.

Understanding Video Resolution

The physical size of a video picture is measured in terms of pixels. A *pixel* is, quite simply, the smallest discrete picture element. The physical size of a pixel is different on different video capture and display devices, so a picture that's 800 pixels wide might be bigger on one computer display than on another. The point, however, is that you measure resolution in pixels; the more pixels in a picture, the higher resolution—and the better the quality.

Standard Versus High Definition

A standard definition television (SDTV) picture has a resolution of 640 pixels wide by 480 pixels tall—or what we call 640×480 resolution. It doesn't matter what physical size the TV screen is; a 15" screen has the same 640×480 resolution as a 35" screen.

Notice that I used the term *standard definition*. This is different from the new high definition television (HDTV) standard—or, to be more precise, *standards*, plural. There are actually several different resolutions used in

HDTV broadcasts and displays, all of which are much higher quality than the older standard resolution picture.

The two most common HD resolutions are 720×1280 (known as *720p resolution*) and 1080×1920 (used in both 1080i and 1080p displays). As you can tell from the numbers, HD packs a lot more pixels in the same screen area, resulting in much sharper pictures.

---

note

HDTV also features a wider screen. A standard definition screen has an aspect ratio of 4:3—that is, the width is 4/3 the height. An HDTV screen has an aspect ratio of 16:9—the width is 16/9 the height. When you view a 16:9 picture on a 4:3 display, you see black bars above and below the picture, a feature known as *letterboxing*.

Are you confused yet? Perhaps Table 4.1 will clear things up a bit; it compares most of the common resolutions you might run into.

Table 4.1   Common Video Resolutions

Resolution (Width×Height)	320×240	480×360	640×480	720×480	1280×720	1920×1080
Description	YouTube standard video	YouTube high quality video	SDTV	SDTV widescreen	720p HDTV	1080i or 1080p HDTV
Aspect ratio	4:3	4:3	4:3	16:9	16:9	16:9
Total number of pixels	76,800	172,800	307,200	345,600	921,600	2,073,600

YouTube Resolution

A high resolution picture would be lost on YouTube viewers because the YouTube site pumps out videos at much lower resolution. In fact, the default YouTube video resolution is a somewhat unimpressive 320×240 pixels—exactly one quarter the total pixels found in an SDTV picture. You can imagine how grainy and pixilated a YouTube video would look if displayed full-screen on a normal television set!

Exploiting Lower Resolution

This leads to a discussion about how the lower resolution affects the content of your YouTube videos. Put simply, when viewing videos in a small, low resolution window, detail gets lost. Don't expect a video crowded with multiple objects to look good on YouTube; in fact, smaller objects in the frame might simply disappear in the background blur.

The best YouTube videos are those that exploit YouTube's low resolution. Don't put small, complex objects on screen; use a large, simple subject instead. What works best? A simple talking head, positioned front and center in the frame. No fancy background, no fiddly details, just the speaker's face big in the frame.

High-Quality Videos

YouTube has recently introduced what it calls *high-quality videos*. These are videos displayed in a larger video window. Not only is the video window larger, it's also a higher resolution: 480×360 pixels. This combination of larger viewing window and higher resolution lets you display more detailed information in your videos; you should plan for all your videos to take advantage of this higher-quality standard.

In my opinion, it's only a matter of time until YouTube moves up to 640×480 resolution. With the future in mind, you might want to create your YouTube videos at 640×480 resolution so that you aren't behind when the change occurs. After all, you can always use a video editing program to downconvert a higher-resolution video to YouTube's current 480×360 pixel resolution. You can't, however, upconvert a lower-resolution video to a higher-resolution format; you can't add more pixels than existed in the first place!

Understanding Video File Formats

A file format is a particular way of encoding digital information. There are lots of different file formats for different uses; for example, Adobe's PDF file format is used to create printable documents, Microsoft's DOC file format is used to create Word documents, and the JPEG file format is used to store digital photographs. Each file format has its own unique attributes and is generally incompatible with other, albeit similar, file formats.

There are several different file formats used to store video information. Each has its own advantages and limitations, so it's important to know the ins and outs of each format before choosing the format you want to record in—in particular, the compression used and the audio/video quality that results.

With that said, you might have little choice in file format. That's because many video cameras record in just one or two formats; not all formats are always available. To that end, YouTube doesn't accept uploads in all formats, so consider that as well.

note

A *container format* is a file format that holds different types of data within the file. These formats, such as the Audio Video Interleave (AVI) and RealVideo formats, contain not only the underlying audio and video, but also metadata about the source material—chapter information, subtitles, and such.

Table 4.2 compares and contrasts the major video file formats. We examine each format in more depth following the table.

Table 4.2   Popular Video File Formats

File Format	Extension	Characteristics
Audio Video Interleave	`.avi`	Container format that can store data encoded in a variety of codecs.
DivX	`.divx`	High-quality codec with equally high compression; popular for Internet use.
Digital Video (DV)	`.dv`	Format used in many consumer video cameras.
Flash Video	`.flv`	Format used by YouTube to serve videos on its site.
H.264	`.mpg, .mp4`	A type of encoding used in some MPEG-4 files; more efficient than normal MPEG-4 codec; used in all iTunes video downloads.
MPEG-1	`.mpg`	Commonly used in digital video cameras.
MPEG-2	`.mpg`	Used in broadcast-quality television and some digital satellite services.
MPEG-4	`.mpg, .mp4`	Most recent version of the MPEG format, optimized for both high definition and Internet video.
QuickTime	`.mov, .qt`	Apple's proprietary audio/video format.
RealVideo	`.rm, .rv`	Media file format used by RealPlayer; the RealMedia format (RM) can contain either audio or video files.
Windows Media Video (WMV)	`.wmv`	Microsoft's proprietary digital video file format.
Xvid	`.xvid`	Similar to the competing DivX codec; a subset of the MPEG-4 file format.

AVI

AVI is an older, Windows-only format, still widely used today. It is a container format, which means it can contain videos encoded with a number of different codecs, combined with metadata about the video's contents. For example, a consumer digital camcorder might record movies in DV format but save those movies in an AVI file. In that instance, the AVI file would contain information about the videos—date and time recorded, length, and so on.

DivX

The DivX codec is a subset of the MPEG-4 format. It uses a form of lossy MPEG-4 compression to compress lengthy video files into small sizes while maintaining relatively high-playback quality. Because of its high compression and high-quality characteristics, DivX is a popular format for sending video files over the Internet. It supports video resolutions up to 1080 HD.

DV

Many digital camcorders use the DV format, particularly those that use Mini DV cassettes. It's a lossy format, even though it doesn't create particularly small files.

DV format video is typically enclosed in some type of container file format, such as AVI or QuickTime. Because it encodes video at the full standard frame rate of 30 frames per second, you can edit videos encoded in the DV format on a frame-by-frame basis.

Flash Video

Flash video is the file format used by YouTube to deliver all its videos. The Flash video format (.flv extension) works with the Adobe Flash Player, which is the basis of the YouTube video player.

FLV files consist of not only the video file, but also a short header and other metadata. The video itself is encoded in an interleaved format.

H.264

The H.264 format, like the DivX format, is a subset of the MPEG-4 format. H.264, also known as *Advanced Video Coding*, is well suited for dealing with high-definition video, such as HDTV broadcasts and Blu-ray Discs. It encodes high-quality video at relatively low bit rates, which results in smaller file sizes—that is particularly important, given the huge native file sizes of high-definition video. All YouTube videos, as well as all videos available on Apple's iTunes Store for PC and iPod playback, use the H.264 codec.

note

The H.264 codec provides similar video quality to MPEG-2 videos recorded at twice the bit rate.

MPEG

Perhaps the most popular video codec today is the MPEG codec—or to be precise, one of several MPEG codecs. The first MPEG codec, MPEG-1, originated as an audio/video compression standard for Video CDs (VCDs). The VCD disc format has been lost to the tides of time, but subsequent iterations of the MPEG codec have become de facto industry standards.

---

note

MPEG stands for *Motion Pictures Expert Group*, a committee that sets international standards for the digital encoding of audio and video. The original MPEG-1 codec is the basis of the popular MP3 audio codec.

There are three primary MPEG codecs, dubbed MPEG-1, MPEG-2, and MPEG-4. Each codec offers progressively better audio/video quality at progressively higher-compression rates—which results in better picture and sound in smaller-sized files. Here's how the MPEG formats compare:

- **MPEG-1**—This is the original MPEG format, used originally in the now extinct VCD format. Some digital camcorders still use it because it creates small, easily transferrable video files; the video quality, however, is only about VHS level. Because of the resulting small file sizes, MPEG-1 remains somewhat popular for posting clips on the Internet.

- **MPEG-2**—This later version of the MPEG standard produces much higher quality audio and video than the original MPEG-1 format, while maintaining small(ish) file sizes. It's commonly used in commercial DVDs, digital satellite broadcasts, TiVo and other digital video recorders, and some broadcast television applications. Despite its lossy nature, the picture quality of the MPEG-1 format is close to that of the DV format.

- **MPEG-4**—This is the latest iteration of the MPEG standard, designed with both the Internet and high-definition video in mind. It produces higher-quality video in smaller-sized files, using improved coding efficiency. It's used in many newer digital camcorders, some digital satellite systems, broadcast HDTV, and streaming Internet videos. There are a number of other formats that can be considered subsets of MPEG-4, including H.264 and DivX; both of these codecs build on and extend the basic MPEG-4 compression.

> **note**
>
> Are you wondering about the missing MPEG-3 format? Experts initially devel-oped MPEG-3 for high-definition video but abandoned it when they realized that they could extend MPEG-2 for that purpose.

QuickTime Movie

The QuickTime Movie format is Apple's proprietary video format, used in Apple's QuickTime media player. It works on both the Mac OS and Windows.

RealVideo

The RealVideo format (part of the larger RealMedia family of formats, which also includes RealAudio) is designed for streaming video content over the Internet. To enhance the speed of streaming, this is a heavily compressed format, resulting in lower-quality video than possible with some other formats.

Windows Media Video

The WMV format is Microsoft's proprietary video format, playable with Microsoft's Windows Media Player. Microsoft claims that the bit rate is twice that of MPEG-4. The result is better video quality, but with larger-sized files.

Xvid

Xvid is another variation of the MPEG-4 format and competes with the similar DivX codec. Unlike the DivX codec, which comes at a price, the Xvid codec is freely distributed, which makes it the format of choice for many Internet users.

Choosing the Right File Format for YouTube

The first thing to know about creating videos for YouTube is which file for-mat YouTube uses. For what it's worth, YouTube stores and serves its videos in Flash Video (FLV) format, using H.264 compression. That said, you can't upload your videos in the Flash format; YouTube converts your videos to this format after you upload them.

Instead, you upload your videos to YouTube in your choice of the MPEG-4 QuickTime or Windows Media Video file format. After you upload your files, YouTube automatically converts them to FLV files.

---

note

Learn more about uploading videos in Chapter 9, "Uploading Your Videos to YouTube."

But file format isn't the only important technical issue to keep in mind. Resolution and frame rate also affect the ultimate quality of your videos when they play on YouTube. In particular, if you upload your videos at too high a resolution, YouTube automatically downconverts them to 320×240 or 480×320 resolution. Unfortunately, YouTube's downconversion often results in grainy or pixelated images. It's far better to create or convert videos yourself at the proper resolution.

That said, if you upload at too low a resolution, YouTube cannot convert your video to higher-resolution formats. For example, a video uploaded at 320×240 won't look good in YouTube's optional 480×320 player window. You want to upload your video in at least 480×320 resolution—or, to be future-proof, at full 640×480 resolution.

So, what are the best settings to use when creating or converting videos? Here's what I recommend:

- MPEG-4 format video with either the DivX or Xvid codec
- MP3 format audio
- 640×480 resolution
- Frame rate of 30 frames per second (FPS)

---

note

Unless you have a Director account, available to professional directors (or aspiring professionals), YouTube also requires that your videos be less than 10 minutes long and smaller than 100MB in file size.

Converting Existing Videos to YouTube Format

When creating a new video from scratch, it's easy to configure your recording device to use the settings just recommended. But what do you do if you want to upload an existing video that's in a different format?

The task of converting videos from one format to another is the province of a video converter program. This type of software automatically does video file format conversion and in the process can convert files from one resolution or size to another. If you have a lot of existing videos you want to upload to YouTube, you need one of these programs. Some of the most popular video conversion programs include

- AVS Video Tools (www.avsmedia.com/VideoTools/)
- M²Convert Professional (www.m2solutionsinc.com/m2convert-pro.htm)
- Movavi VideoSuite (www.movavi.com/suite/)
- Power Video Converter (www.apussoft.com)
- RER Video Converter (www.rersoft.com/videoconverter.htm)
- VIDEOzilla (www.videozilla.net)
- Xilisoft Video Converter (www.xilisoft.com/video-converter.html)

Using one of these converter programs is typically as easy as selecting the file to convert, choosing an output format, and then clicking the Convert button. Other settings (such as resolution or frame rate) are sometimes available, but the basic conversion process is most often a one-click operation.

The Big Picture

There's a lot you could learn about video technologies, but you don't have to knock yourself out—unless you really want to. Just remember to shoot in MPEG-4 format at 640×480 resolution. You can then upload said files to the YouTube site, which will automatically convert them to 320×240 and 480×360 resolution FLV format. The conversion happens in the background on the YouTube site; you don't have to deal with it. ■

5

Shooting Webcam Videos

There are three ways to record a video for YouTube. If you have a big budget, you can go with a professional recording, complete with lights, sound, professional-grade video cameras, and the like. If that's outside your budget, and it probably is, you can record with a consumer-grade camcorder. And if even that sounds pricey to you, you can record your videos with a standard computer webcam.

In fact, recording YouTube videos with a webcam has some benefits, chief among them the immediacy and flexibility that come from the format. And it's a low cost solution: You can purchase a webcam for as little as $30.

Should you record your business videos with a webcam? And if so, how do you do it? That's what we cover in this chapter.

Understanding Webcam Video

A *webcam* is a small camera, typically with an accompanying miniature microphone, which attaches to any computer via USB port. As you can see in Figure 5.1, most webcams fit on top of your monitor screen; some notebook PCs come with a webcam built in.

FIGURE 5.1
Logitech's QuickCam Pro 9000 webcam, mounted on top of an LCD monitor.

Given the webcam's small footprint, it is a relatively unobtrusive way to shoot YouTube videos. Also, when attached to a notebook PC operating on battery power, a webcam lets you shoot videos just about anywhere—a truly portable solution.

Webcams, however, do not produce the highest-quality video and audio. Typical lower-priced webcams shoot video at a resolution of 640×480, but with a lower-quality lens that neither works well in darkened conditions nor reproduces especially sharp images. Higher-priced webcams, such as Logitech's QuickCam Pro 9000, can capture images at 1600×1200 high definition resolution, and also include a higher-quality lens. Still, if you want broadcast-quality video, a webcam is the least satisfactory of the three different shooting options.

The audio you get with a webcam is not the best either. In most instances, you'll be speaking into a small microphone embedded within the webcam itself; the farther away you are from the webcam, the less clear your voice recording will come out. (Some webcams include a separate clip-on microphone, for just this reason.) And, let's be honest, this isn't studio-quality audio here; webcam audio is barely satisfactory for voice, and not for much of anything else.

With that said, the lower-quality picture and sound inherent in webcam capture lends your webcam videos a sense of immediacy; the effect is one of raw, "you are there," citizen journalism. The effect is also one of direct-ness, a one-on-one communication between the speaker and the viewer, with little in the way of fancy production in between.

Figure 5.2 shows a screenshot from a webcam video I shot in my local cof-feehouse. As you can see, the raw nature of the webcam makes for a per-sonal effect. As you can also see, shooting with a webcam puts you at the mercy of your environment; in this instance, a bright side light coming from a nearby window. You might not have this problem when you're shooting in your office, but it is something to watch out for when shoot-ing on the go.

FIGURE 5.2

A webcam video shot "in the field" at a local coffeehouse.

Webcams can capture video and audio to your hard drive, typically in AVI (Audio Video Interleave) file format, using the software that comes with most webcam packages. Webcams can also stream live video over the Internet, which is common when using the webcam to chat via instant messaging or in chat rooms—but is also useful when you want to upload videos directly from your webcam to YouTube, a process we dis-cuss later in this chapter.

When a Webcam Makes Sense

So, when might you want to shoot your business videos with a webcam? Let's look at some of the different types of videos that benefit from web-cam capture.

Creating a Video Blog

The most common use of webcam video is in the creation of video blogs or *vlogs*. Think of a video blog as a video version of a traditional text blog—an opportunity for you or someone from your company to offer regular personal insights into business trends and events.

With a video blog, the low-quality immediacy of a webcam works to your advantage. If you shoot a vlog in a professional recording studio, the result is often too slick for the viewer to take seriously. You almost need the nonprofessional nature of a webcam to give your vlog legitimacy.

In addition, if you're vlogging on a frequent basis, it's a lot easier to plug in a webcam than it is to set up a camcorder, lights, and an external microphone. When you have something to say, just plug in, turn on, and start talking. The ease-of-use alone should encourage more frequent vlogging—which is a good thing.

Reporting from the Road or Special Events

A webcam is essential when you're traveling and still need to contribute to your company's vlog or YouTube videos. It doesn't matter where you are; all you need is a webcam and a notebook computer, and you're good to go.

This makes sense, of course, if you're a traveling salesperson or an executive with a busy travel schedule. It's also great when you're attending special events: trade shows, conferences, seminars, and the like. With your webcam and notebook PC in tow, you can contribute up-to-the-minute reporting from just about anywhere, including the convention floor or conference room. Your equipment does not limit you at all.

Responding to Immediate Issues

In the unfortunate event of a serious event hitting your company, you can immediately address the issue with the use of a quick-and-dirty webcam video. When disaster strikes, you want to get in front of the issue and minimize the bad PR. What better way than a personal response from the company president, recorded live to webcam?

This is another instance where a professionally produced video would be counterproductive. It would appear too impersonal and take too long to create. You can create a webcam video a lot faster, and the results speak more directly to interested viewers.

Capturing Customer Testimonials

Finally, if you're using customer testimonials as part of your online marketing mix, there's no better way to capture those testimonials than via webcam. First, you get the immediacy effect; your customers will appear more "real" on webcam than they might in a studio. Second, it's an inexpensive approach because customers can create their own videos! Just send them a complimentary webcam, have one of your tech support folks talk them through installation and operation, and let your customers shoot themselves at their convenience. Instead of laying out tens of thousands of dollars in travel expenses and professional video production, you're out about a hundred bucks for a webcam. What's not to like?

Tips for Shooting an Effective Webcam Video

If you decide to use webcam video as part of your YouTube video mix, how do you best take advantage of the medium? In other words, how do you make the best-looking and most-effective webcam video possible?

Make It Immediate

Webcam video works best when it conveys immediacy. That means you don't want it to look *too* professional. It's okay to make a few verbal mistakes and leave them in the video. Make it look as if you're speaking off the cuff, even if you are working from a script. You want your video to have the feel of a deskside chat, just you talking directly to the audience. Nothing fancy, nothing too polished. Just you and the webcam, one-to-one.

Keep It Simple

Webcam video is typically of lower quality than other types of video you might shoot. You need to keep the picture simple; fiddly details are lost in the lower-resolution picture.

What works best? Just you, close to the webcam, and talking directly to the camera. Don't try to fit two people into the frame; doing that on a webcam just looks silly. And don't even think about moving around: Sit still, directly in front of the camera, and keep your movements to a minimum. Action captured via webcam often looks jerky.

Simplicity counts in terms of visual composition. Sit in front of a plain background of either white or light gray; a busy background is distracting on YouTube. You should also avoid overly bright background colors, which can also be distracting.

In terms of composition, move up close to the camera. Although you might be tempted to show yourself from the waist up, that shot makes your face too small for the YouTube viewing window. Go for a head-and-shoulders shot or move even closer for a pure headshot. Remember, it's you talking directly to the viewer—so make sure the viewer can see you!

Watch the Lighting

Most webcams don't handle extremes in lighting very well. For example, you'll get a lousy picture if the room light is too dark. So, you want lots of light—as long as it's shining on your face. What you don't want is back-light shining from behind you, which tricks the webcam into darkening the picture and throwing your face into shadow. You need good lighting on your face, even if that means moving around some room lights or using an external photoflood positioned behind the webcam.

tip
If you're not sure whether you have the right light, shoot a test video and see how it looks—before you upload your real video to the YouTube site.

Minimize the Background Noise

Most webcams don't include a high-quality microphone, which means that the sound you get on a webcam video is often of lower quality than you might want. You can compensate by sitting as close to the webcam as possible and speaking loudly and clearly. Don't mumble and don't whisper; enunciate as if you're speaking to an auditorium full of people.

You should also know that the webcam will pick up any background noise in the room, which can be distracting to YouTube viewers. Turn off any noisy mechanical or electronic devices, including fans, coffee machines, printers—you name it. (Air conditioners are particularly noisy, with their low humming.) And make sure that anyone else in the room with you stays quiet!

Uploading Webcam Video to YouTube

Another nice thing about shooting with a webcam is that YouTube makes it easy to upload webcam videos. You can save your webcam video to a standard video file and then upload it, or you can use YouTube's Quick Capture feature to upload a video as you record it, in real time. The latter method is quite easy to use, even if it doesn't allow you the luxury of editing the videos you record.

Uploading Webcam Video Files

The standard approach to uploading webcam video is to take your time while recording, using multiple takes if necessary, and then to save your results in an AVI or similar format file. Most webcams come with software for capturing video in this fashion; follow the instructions to save your video files.

From there, you can edit the webcam video files using a video-editing program and then upload the resulting file to the YouTube site. We cover this method of uploading in more detail in Chapter 9, "Uploading Your Videos to YouTube"; turn there for more information.

note

Learn more about editing your webcam videos in Chapter 8, "Editing and Enhancing Your Videos."

Uploading Live Webcam Video

An alternative to uploading video files is to upload your webcam video as you shoot it, live from your webcam. This second method of uploading webcam videos utilizes YouTube's Quick Capture feature. Here's how it works.

note

When you use Quick Capture to upload live webcam videos to YouTube, you don't have the opportunity to edit those videos. Whatever you record is what YouTube shows, warts and all.

With your webcam connected and running, click the Upload Videos link on any YouTube page. When the Video Upload page appears, as shown in Figure 5.3, enter a title, description, video category, and tags for the video. With this basic information added, click the Use Quick Capture button.

FIGURE 5.3
Entering information about a webcam video.

This displays the Quick Capture page, shown in Figure 5.4. Pull down the list boxes at the top of the Record Video window to select your webcam video and audio options; you should now see the picture from your webcam in the Record Video window.

FIGURE 5.4
Recording a live webcam video with Quick Capture.

note

If, when you first access the Quick Capture page, you see an Adobe Flash Player Settings dialog box, click the Allow button.

To start recording, click the Record button. When you finish recording your video, click the Stop button. At this point you have the option of clicking Cancel to delete your recording, Preview to view a preview of the video you just recorded, or Save to save your video to the YouTube site. When you click Save, YouTube automatically uploads the video to the site and displays the Upload Complete page. Your video will be available for viewing in a few minutes.

tip

If you don't like what you just recorded, click the Cancel button and start over.

The Big Picture

The easiest way to create videos for YouTube is to use an inexpensive computer webcam. A webcam lets you capture videos from just about anywhere, with an immediacy often lacking in other types of video capture.

YouTube lets you upload webcam videos in one of two ways. You can save your webcam video to a video file and upload that file, or you can use the Quick Capture feature to upload live video as you record it—no editing necessary (or possible)! ■

Shooting Semi-Pro Videos

As you learned in the previous chapter, the easiest and most afford-able way to create a YouTube video is to use a computer webcam. But webcam video is low quality and limiting, not ideal for all business uses. How, then, can you shoot a more professional-looking YouTube video without spending the bucks for truly professional production?

For many businesses, the best bang for the buck comes from using consumer-grade video equipment, but in a professional manner. We're talking about the kinds of video camcorder you can find at your local Best Buy or Circuit City, augmented by sophisticated video editing software and the appropriate accessories. The resulting videos can look almost identical to professionally made videos but without expensive professional involvement.

Understanding Consumer Video Equipment

When I was a kid, my dad shot home movies using a Super 8 film camera. The movies were about what you would expect—lots of cute, little kids mugging about in a dark, shaky, poorly focused little film.

Well, all that's changed. Thanks to today's digital video technology, you can now shoot videos in high resolution and edit them on your home computer. The results are often indistinguishable from what you'd get from a professional video production house, complete with sophisticated editing and special effects. And the costs are no more, in today's terms, than what my dad spent back when I was a youth.

It's amazing: Digital video recording lets you use your PC as a movie-editing studio to create sophisticated videos for YouTube distribution.

How Camcorders Work

The key to successful semi-pro video production is to start with a digital camcorder. Fortunately, now that older analog VHS camcorders have been relegated to the garbage bin or to eBay auctions, virtually every camcorder sold today records in a digital format.

The nice things about today's digital camcorders are that they're easy enough for even an executive to use and produce high-quality results. Just point the camcorder, press the Record button, and zoom into the shot. Some higher-end camcorders feature image stabilization technology, so shaky pictures are a thing of the past. And, with today's digital recording formats, the movies you shoot are at professional-quality levels.

---

note

The best camcorders available today feature 16:9 aspect ratio picture, interchangeable lenses, a variety of scene effects, and high definition recording. These camcorders are comparable to the ones the pros use, but they're available to regular consumers—albeit at high prices.

Let's start with the basics. As you can tell from its name, a camcorder is actually two devices in one, combining a video *camera* and video *recorder* into a single unit. The camera part of the unit senses the image, and the recorder section records it.

In the camera part of the camcorder, the process starts when the image is seen through the camera's lens. The higher quality the lens, the more light that passes through it without distortion of the image.

The image as seen by the lens is beamed onto a *charge-coupled device* (*CCD*), which is an electronic chip that captures the light falling on it and converts the light to electrical signals. Most consumer-level camcorders use a single CCD to capture the video image. Some high-end camcorders, however, use three CCDs, one for each of the primary colors (red, green, and blue), which provides better detail and color. Most professional video cameras use a three-CCD design.

The CCD generates the digital signal transmitted to the camcorder's recording section. Depending on the type of camcorder, this might be a tape-based recorder (typically in the MiniDV format), a recordable DVD, recordable flash memory, or even a hard disk like the one found in your computer.

Because the audio and video signals are recorded digitally, you can transfer them (via either an IEEE 1394 FireWire or USB connection) to any personal computer and then edit them using digital movie-editing software. When you record digitally, edit digitally, and then transfer the digital files to YouTube, you keep a fully digital signal path, which results in extremely high-quality picture and sound.

Examining Camcorder Formats

If you used a camcorder a decade or so ago, chances are it used either the VHS or VHS-C tape format. Both of these formats were analog formats with limited image resolution. Today, however, virtually every camcorder records in a digital format, capable of much better picture quality than was delivered in the past.

There are several recording formats available for you to choose from today. The most common formats include the following:

- **MiniDV**—This is the most common and lowest-priced digital camcorder format available today. It records broadcast-quality (500+ lines of resolution) digital video in the DV format, using small, low price cassettes that are about 1/12 the size of a standard VHS tape. Use MiniDV for optimal compatibility with video-editing programs and other equipment.

- **HDV**—This is a high definition version of the MiniDV format and is found on some higher-priced high definition camcorders. HDV uses either standard MiniDV cassettes or special HDV cassettes but produces either 720p or 1080i resolution along with Dolby Digital surround sound.

- **DVD**—DVD camcorders don't use tape at all; they record directly to DVDs, using small (8cm diameter) discs that record in the DVD-R, DVD-RW, or DVD+RW format. Depending on the picture quality level you select, each disc can hold between 20 to 60 minutes of video. Assuming that your home DVD player can accept these mini discs, the advantage of this format is that you don't have to bother transferring your movies from tape to DVD at a later point. DVD camcorders record video in MPEG-2 format.

- **HDD**—In this instance, HDD stands for *hard disk drive*. HDD cam-corders record directly to a built-in miniature hard disk drive, just like the kind you have on your personal computer. Current models incorporate hard drives from 30GB to 120GB in size. It takes about 4GB of storage for one hour of standard definition video at the high-est quality setting, whereas the lower-quality "economy" setting needs less than 1GB for each hour of video. HDD camcorders record video in MPEG-2 format.

- **Flash memory**—These camcorders record directly to a CompactFlash, SD/MMC, or Memory Stick flash memory device in MPEG-2 format. Because of the small size of the storage card, these are typically compact camcorders.

Which is the best recording format to use? If you're intending to transfer your videos to a PC for editing, I recommend an HDD camcorder. It's easy to transfer digital video files from a camcorder's hard drive to a PC's hard drive via either a FireWire or USB connection.

note

Other, now obsolete, digital video formats include Digital8 and MicroMV.

Choosing a Camcorder

You don't have to spend a lot of money to buy a camcorder. As it always does, developing technology helps to bring you better performance at a significantly lower price than you would have paid just a few years ago. The challenge is picking the right camcorder for your needs.

Even the lowest-priced camcorders, like the JVC HDD model shown in Figure 6.1, take surprisingly good pictures. Most of the picture quality is in the file format itself, rather than in the additional features in a particular camcorder. This means that many people shooting videos for YouTube can get by with a simple $250 camcorder, no problem. But higher-priced models are available and worthy of your consideration.

The more money you spend on a camcorder, the more bells and whistles you get. In particular, a bigger budget buys you one or more of the fol-lowing: compact size, ease of use, bigger zoom lens, special features (such as transition effects, night-vision shooting, and so on), and higher-quality performance.

FIGURE 6.1

JVC's affordable GZ-MG330 hard disk camcorder.

After you get beyond budget camcorders, you should look for a model that includes a good quality zoom lens, image stabilization (to keep your pictures steady, even if your hands aren't), various automatic exposure modes, and some sort of built-in video editing. This last feature lets you perform in-camera edits between scenes, including audio dubbing, fade in and out, and other special effects.

You should also pay particular attention to the camcorder's image-sensing system. Most lower-priced camcorders use a single CCD to capture the video image. Higher-priced models use a three-CCD system that optically splits the image and feeds color-filtered versions of the scene to three CCD sensors, one for each color: red, green, and blue. Naturally, a three-CCD camera delivers better color than a single-CCD model.

In addition, a bigger CCD reproduces a better quality picture: 1/3" CCDs are better than 1/6" CCDs. For even better picture quality, look for a camcorder with progressive scan technology and true 16:9 framing for film-like results.

Prosumer and High Definition Camcorders

Most consumer-level camcorders are small enough to hold in the palm of your hand. But if you're interested in independent filmmaking or just want higher performance, you have to move to a larger model. These camcorders, called *prosumer* models, are often big enough to require a shoulder rest. The Canon XL2 in Figure 6.2 is one example of a prosumer camcorder. They look, feel, and perform just like the type of camcorder you see TV news crews or independent filmmakers lugging around.

FIGURE 6.2

Canon's XL2 prosumer camcorder.

Many prosumer camcorders let you use interchangeable lenses for more shooting versatility and shoot in the 16:9 widescreen format. More importantly, they come with a bevy of automatic recording modes and manual adjustments that enable you to custom-tailor your movies to a variety of shooting styles and situations. Their picture quality is second to none, especially under difficult lighting conditions.

The best camcorders today move beyond the traditional standard definition format to record movies in true high definition video. An HDV camcorder, such as the Sony model shown in Figure 6.3, offers all the features of a similar-level standard definition camcorder, but with the capability of recording high definition signals onto a MiniDV tape or hard disk. Depending on the camera, recording is in either the 720p or 1080i format, both of which should be playable on any HDTV-capable television.

FIGURE 6.3

Sony's HDR-CX7 high definition HDD camcorder.

Naturally, an HDV camcorder shoots in the 16:9 aspect ratio, which is part of the high definition format. You can also record Dolby Digital surround sound, although you'll probably need an external surround sound microphone to do so.

Selecting Essential Accessories

One of the keys to shooting more professional videos is to take advantage of available accessories such as tripods, lighting kits, and the like. For example, you get a better-quality picture when you put more light in the lens, so it makes sense to use auxiliary lighting via either a single camera-mounted light, such as the one shown in Figure 6.4, or a full multiple-flood setup. Using professional-quality lighting is one of the easiest ways to make your videos look more professional.

FIGURE 6.4

The Sunpak Readylite camera-mounted video light.

You can enhance the quality of your sound by using a better microphone than the one in the camcorder. It's an unfortunate fact that most camcorders include a low-quality mic. In addition, your subject is typically half a room away, which does not bode well for quality sound.

To enhance the audio in your videos, look for a camcorder that lets you connect an external microphone. You can choose from boom mics, stereo mics, surround sound mics, and even lavaliere or lapel mics (such as the one shown in Figure 6.5)—just like the pros use. Just make sure that the mic you choose has the same connector as found on your camera—they're not all the same.

tip

If you have a large crew, my recommendation is to use a boom mic. Otherwise, go with a wireless lavaliere mic that clips onto the front of the speaker's shirt or tie.

And don't forget stability. Only amateur movies (and professional movies trying for an artsy "shaky cam" effect) bounce around like a monkey on caffeine. You need a way to steady your camera when you shoot, which can be as simple as a monopod or tripod (such as the one shown in Figure 6.6) or a fancy shoulder mount with some sort of motion-stabilization rig.

FIGURE 6.5

Audio-Technica's ES943C lavaliere microphone.

FIGURE 6.6

The sturdy DV-6000 video tripod from Velbon.

Put it all together, and you end up with a steady, well-lit video with intelligible sound. That's a far cry from the dark, shaky Super 8 movies of my youth—and a good reason to invest in all these fun, little gadgets.

Building a Computer for Video Editing

The other essential component in creating a semi-pro video is the personal computer you use to edit your videos. It's important, then, to build a computer system that has the horsepower necessary for this demanding task.

Video editing is the second-most demanding operation you can do on your PC. (The most demanding activity is playing games, believe it or not.) It takes a lot of processing power, memory, and hard disk storage to edit and process full-motion video, and most older and lower-priced PCs simply aren't up to the task. It might mean, depending on your unit, that you have some upgrading to do.

So, what kind of PC do you need for video editing? If you're an Apple user, there's no better computer for video editing than a Mac Pro. This machine has all the horsepower and features you need to do all sorts of fancy video editing without even breaking a sweat. If you're a Windows user, you have a lot more choices. To start with, you want to go with the fastest, most powerful processor you can afford—at least 3GHz, faster if you can get it.

Memory is an important part of the equation, too. The bare minimum required for video editing today is 2GB, although you should go for more if you can.

You also need lots of hard disk space with a fast hard disk. Perhaps the best way to go is to add a dedicated external hard disk just for your video editing. Make sure the hard drive connects via FireWire because FireWire is faster for this type of data transfer than USB.

When it comes to hard disk storage, bigger is better. For example, if you shoot a standard definition video at 5:1 compression, you need 3.6MB for every second of video you shoot. That's almost 13GB for a full hour of video. After you have a few videos (or even a few differently edited versions of the same video) on your hard disk, the space used starts getting big. For this reason, consider a 500GB or 1TB (terabyte) drive for your video storage. You can't have too much hard disk space.

---

tip

When calculating the necessary hard disc space, factor in the amount of raw video you have, not just the length of the final edited video. It's easy for your raw material to be ten times or more as long as your final product!

Obviously, your computer needs to have a FireWire connection because that's how most digital camcorders connect. Your camcorder manufacturer might use the consumer electronics term *iLink* or the more technical *IEEE 1394*, but it's still FireWire.

Finally, consider what type of monitor you'll be using. Here again, bigger is better—at least 20" diagonal. Although it might seem like overkill to use a big widescreen monitor to edit little 320×240 YouTube videos, all the components of your video-editing program take up a lot of screen space. Plus, you want to produce your videos for a future 640×480 YouTube environment, which requires a bigger screen to edit at full size.

When a Semi-Pro Video Makes Sense

We've spent a lot of time discussing how to assemble the right equipment to shoot a semi-pro YouTube video. But just when does this type of video make sense for your business?

Video Blogs

In the previous chapter, we discussed using a webcam to create your video blog (called a *vlog*). Even though webcam video has the immediacy that defines such a vlog, the webcam's lower-quality picture and sound might work against any professional image you're trying to impart.

You can create much better looking, and better sounding, videos with a low-cost consumer camcorder and still maintain the immediacy necessary for a legitimate vlog. The key here is to keep your set—what's in front of and behind the subject in the video—spare and functional. No elaborate decorations, no fancy lighting, just the subject speaking into a camcorder. The result is a clearer, less jerky picture than what you can accomplish with a webcam but still with the personal one-to-one effect.

To shoot a video blog, all you need is a camcorder and a tripod. If you don't have a separate camera operator, make sure your camcorder has a wireless remote control so that you can turn it on and off from in front of the camera. You can shoot under natural light or augment the room light with a camcorder-mounted external light. It might be a good idea to use a lavaliere microphone for better sound, if your camcorder has a mic input.

---

tip

When you're shooting yourself with a camcorder, swivel the LCD viewfinder 180° so that you can watch yourself from in front of the camera while you're record-ing. (But make sure you look into the lens when you're recording, not into the viewfinder!)

Executive Messages

Messages to consumers or employees from the executive office look more professional, and thus more authoritative, when shot with a camcorder versus the less professional look of a webcam video. With a quality cam-corder, the executive doesn't have to venture into a professional recording studio to say his piece; recording the message can take place in the execu-tive's office or corporate boardroom.

Although some executives might think that they deserve professional video production, complete with flattering lighting and a makeup person, the reality is that you can achieve similar results with a well-conceived semi-production. The key here is to make the executive think it's a profes-sional production, which also helps to improve your overall production values. Invest in some external lighting (which improves the video's look), hook up a wireless lavaliere microphone (which improves the video's sound), and have an assistant dab some pancake on the exec's shiny fore-head (which improves the executive's look). Mount the camcorder on a tripod, have enough staffers nearby to handle any contingencies, and use a laptop computer near the camera lens as a teleprompter. The exec should feel pampered enough, and the resulting video quality should be good enough to please everyone involved.

Product Demonstrations

You don't need a fancy video recording studio to shoot effective product demonstrations. All you need is a quality consumer-grade camcorder, an adequate lighting setup, a boom or lavaliere mic, and the patience to shoot the same sequence from multiple angles. The equipment should give you a quality video, and the multiple shots give you choices to use when you edit the video.

One of the common pitfalls of semi-pro product demonstrations is the sound. It's easy to get a quality picture (assuming that you're not shooting under straight room lighting), but the sound trips up a lot of inexperienced producers. The mistake is to think the camcorder's built-in microphone can do the job, which it probably can't; it captures all the sounds in the room, including the ancillary sounds of the crew and the product itself. You'll get much better sound by using multiple external microphones: a lavaliere mic to isolate the demonstrator's voice and a boom mic to capture product sounds. You can mix the two soundtracks for optimal effect when you edit the video.

On-the-Scene Reports

Let's not forget the portable nature of a camcorder: A handheld model can shoot practically anywhere. This, of course, makes a camcorder ideal for shooting outside the office, in just about any location.

Consider, for example, shooting an on-the-road video, with a cameraman accompanying the host to various locations. Perhaps you need an outdoor demonstration of your product, or want to file a report from a trade show or conference, or document a visit to a remote office. You can shoot any of these videos with a simple camcorder, no optional equipment necessary—although an external mic and camera light might be useful if the situation allows.

Shooting a Semi-Pro Video

What's the best way to shoot a semi-pro video? It depends on your situation, but basic techniques hold in any instance.

Shooting in the Office

When you're shooting indoors in familiar surroundings, you have a nice home court advantage—and a lot of control over the situation. You can take advantage of this situation to shoot extremely high-quality videos. All you need is the right equipment, a little preparation, and a lot of patience.

As to equipment, here's what I recommend:

- High-quality camcorder with external microphone input
- Tripod
- Lavaliere or boom microphone
- External video light—either a camera-mounted light or a set of separate photofloods

Set up your equipment in front of the subject. Set the subject in front of a plain, nondistracting background; if you can, choose a background color that contrasts with the subject's clothing or the color of the product you're shooting. Mic the subject with a lavaliere mic or, if you have a dedicated sound person, use a boom mic positioned above and to the front of the subject.

---

tip

If you have the space and budget, consider investing in a roll or two of seamless photographic background paper and accompanying stands. Also good are patterned muslin or cloth backdrops, all of which you can find at better photo retailers.

If your subject is reading from a script, enter the script into a notebook computer and position the computer either just below or to the side of the camera lens. I like to use PowerPoint as a makeshift teleprompter. Make sure the display font is large enough for the subject to comfortably read it from across the room, and that you have someone to scroll down the text in the program as the subject reads it.

After everything is set up (and take your time doing this; rushing things can create unsatisfactory results), run through the shoot a few times for practice. When everyone—including both the subject and the cameraman—is ready, shoot the video for real. If something goes wrong, stop the shoot and do another take. In fact, you should shoot several takes and use the best of the bunch in your final video.

You might also want to shoot the video again from another angle, or with close-ups on the product, the demonstrator's hands, or whatever. This gives you a library of shots to use during the editing process; cutting away to a close-up, for example, helps to increase the visual interest of the video. The key is to give yourself enough options to best edit the final video. Don't paint yourself into a box with a single take of a static shot.

Shooting Outside the Office

When you're shooting a video in the field, you're operating under less than ideal conditions. That isn't necessarily a bad thing, but something you need to be prepared for.

The first thing you need to know is that you probably can't use all your fancy equipment. In the worst case scenario, all you'll have is your camcorder, which means using available light and recording audio directly into the camcorder's built-in microphone. You might, under certain conditions, be able to use a camera-mounted video light or an external microphone. (In outdoor shots, I recommend a wireless lavaliere microphone to cut down on background and wind noise.) But if all you get to use is the camcorder itself, be prepared to work under those conditions.

Working in the field means making the most of what you have available. Examine your surroundings to find an appropriate background for your subject. Unlike an in-office shot, going with a plain background might not be the best approach; you might want to capture some of the local flavor in your video, which means shooting with some sort of identifying landmark in the background. Make sure the background doesn't distract from the subject and that you properly frame the subject and the background.

You also need to consider the lighting—both the type of lighting and its originating direction. Indirect lighting is better than direct lighting, which is often harsh and unflattering, and side lighting is better than overhead lighting. You definitely don't want the light to shine directly on the subject's face; it will make him squint. Light directly behind the subject is also bad because you get a backlight effect that puts the subject's face in shadow. The best light comes from the side and is slightly diffused—like what you get on a cloudy day. (Alternatively, use a reflector to bounce sunlight onto the subject from below or from the side.)

tip

If you're shooting outdoors, try to shoot in the early morning or late afternoon—those so-called golden hours when the sun is low on the horizon and has a warmish cast.

Finally, if you have a tripod handy, use it—unless you want the "you are there" type of shaky cam effect. Get everything set up, do a run through or two if time and conditions permit, and then start shooting!

Transferring Videos to Your PC for Editing

After you shoot your video, you need to transfer it to a PC for editing and uploading to YouTube. How you do this depends on the type of camcorder you have and precisely what it is you want to do.

Transferring from a Digital Camcorder

If you have a digital camcorder, connecting your camcorder to your PC is a snap. All you need is an IE1394 FireWire port on your PC. This type of connection is fast enough to handle the huge stream of digital data pour-ing from your DV recorder into your PC.

note
Many low-end camcorders now connect via USB instead of FireWire.

Transferring a video from your camcorder to your PC is typically as easy as pushing a button on your camcorder. Each movie is stored in a sepa-rate digital file. When you transfer the movie, you're actually copying the digital file from your camcorder to your PC, just as you would any other digital file from any storage device. When copied to your PC's hard drive, you can edit the file or upload it to YouTube.

Transferring from an Analog Camcorder

If you have an older VHS, VHS-C, SVHS, 8mm, or Hi8 recorder, the con-nection isn't as simple. That's because you have to convert the analog video from your camcorder to the digital format used by your PC.

To do this, you need to purchase and install an analog-to-digital video capture card in your PC—you can buy one at most computer stores. Plug your camcorder into the jacks in the card, typically using standard RCA connectors, and the card converts the analog signals from your recorder into the digital audio and video your computer understands.

tip
If you don't want to install a new card in your PC, you can get the same func-tionality from an external video capture device, such as Pinnacle Systems' Dazzle Digital Video Creator unit. These devices have standard audio and video input jacks to connect to your camcorder and connect to your PC via USB.

To transfer a movie from your analog camcorder to your PC, you actually play the movie on your camcorder and record it on your PC. This means that the transfer takes place in real time as the movie plays. (This is a lot slower than simply copying a file from a digital camcorder.) As the video transfers to your PC, the analog signals from your camcorder convert into digital audio and video.

Tips for Shooting an Effective Semi-Pro Video

Do you want to shoot a better semi-pro video, one that truly looks profes-sional? Then pay attention to the following tips—they'll help you avoid producing amateurish videos with your new equipment.

Shoot Digitally

This one should go without saying, but I'll say it anyway. I don't care if you are on a tight budget, and your uncle, or the guy down the hall, or whoever has an old camcorder he's willing to let you borrow at no cost. You don't want to shoot on analog tape; the best results come from keeping an all-digital chain. That means using a newer digital video camcorder, period. It doesn't matter whether you shoot on MiniDV tape or hard disk, what does matter is that the video is digital.

Keep the Proper Resolution in Mind

Even if your camcorder is capable of shooting in high definition widescreen video, there's little point in doing so. As you recall from Chapter 4, "Understanding Audio/Video Technology," standard YouTube videos display at substandard 320×240 resolution, with the newer "high quality" videos at a slightly better 480×360 resolution. As such, shooting at anything higher than 640×480 is just a waste of pixels; you would need to substantially downconvert higher-quality video to match YouTube's resolution.

Likewise, shooting in widescreen (16:9) mode merely results in a letterbox video in YouTube's standard aspect ratio (4:3) video player window, which wastes valuable space in the YouTube video window. Shoot at 4:3 ratio to fill the entire YouTube video window.

Use a Tripod

One of the easiest ways to turn a good video into a mediocre one is to shoot it without a tripod. I know, handheld cameras are designed to be handheld, but that doesn't mean they should be. When you hold a camera in your hand, it *moves*; it's impossible for you to hold the camera perfectly still for the three minutes or so of the entire video. The result is a jerky, jumpy picture that looks more like a home movie than a professional video production. That's not what you want.

You obtain better results when you invest in a tripod. Mount the camera on the tripod, and it won't move around anymore. Your picture stays stable and clear, with a much more professional look. A tripod is the first and best investment you can make in your video production capabilities!

Lighting Matters

I've already said it multiple times in this chapter, but it bears repeating: Shooting in available light seldom achieves acceptable results. You can dramatically improve the look of your videos by adding light—augmenting the available light with some sort of external light. This can be a camera-mounted video light, freestanding photofloods, or a full-blown video lighting kit, such as the one shown in Figure 6.7. The key is to get more—and better—light into the shot.

FIGURE 6.7

Smith-Victor's K76 professional studio lighting kit.

Better lighting, by the way, isn't just to get rid of lingering shadows. Most indoor lighting isn't quite white; the color of white varies from light source to light source. Some types of lighting produce a cooler (bluer) white, and others produce a warmer (redder) white. And when the light itself is colored, it affects all the other colors in the shot.

For example, candlelight casts a warm light, almost orange. Incandescent bulbs are also slightly warm, whereas florescent bulbs are cooler—to the point of having a slightly greenish cast. In contrast, studio lighting has a more neutral cast, which is what you want for your videos.

note

You might be able to compensate for different types of lighting in your camcorder. Look for a white balance or color correction control and follow your camcorder's directions for setting a true white level.

Use an External Microphone

All camcorders have a built-in microphone. With most lower-end camcorders, that's the only option you have; you have to use the camcorder's mic for all your audio needs. In contrast, higher-end camcorders come with an external microphone jack to which you can connect most any type of external mic. This is a good thing.

There are two bad things about using a camcorder's internal microphone. First, it's typically not a high-quality mic; the sound quality is mediocre at best. Second, the microphone is on the camcorder, not on the subject—who is often on the other side of the room. That means the subject has to yell just to be picked up by the mic, which also picks up any other sounds between the subject and the camcorder—not the best situation for capturing quality audio.

It's far, far better to mic the subject directly, using a handheld mic, lavaliere mic, or even a boom mic. The keys are to get the mic closer to the subject and to isolate the subject from all other background sounds. You want to clearly hear what the subject is saying, and only what the subject is saying—and the only way to do that is with an external microphone.

Watch the Background

Did you ever notice the background in a professionally shot video? Probably not, and that speaks to the care in which it was chosen. You're not supposed to notice the background; your attention is supposed to focus on the main subject.

The point is that you need to pay particular attention to what's behind the subject in your shot. Don't just point your camera at an executive sitting behind her desk without also examining what's behind that executive. If the background is too busy, it distracts from the subject; the viewer's eyes drift to the background instead of to the person who's talking.

What kinds of backgrounds do you want to avoid? The list includes things such as open windows (especially with people walking by outside!), busy wallpaper, cluttered bookshelves, and just general clutter. It's much better to shoot in front of a plain wall, if you have no other choice.

Even better is to use some sort of professional background. Any good photography store sells seamless background paper, as well as cloth and muslin backgrounds with various unobtrusive patterns. If you do a lot of corporate videos, consider creating your own unique patterned background that incorporates your company's logo, either large or in a smaller repeating pattern.

By the way, the patterned message background is the one favored by politicians, who think it's somehow subliminal to repeat the message du jour behind them at every photo or video opportunity. (Figure 6.8 shows President Bush in front of a typical repeated-logo background; in this instance, for a speech at the National Institutes of Health.) Politicians around the world like to stand in front of their country's flag.

FIGURE 6.8

President Bush in front of a repeated logo for the National Institutes of Health—get the message?

A Little Movement Is Good...

Not all semi-pro videos need to be static. One of the advantages of using a camcorder is that, unlike a webcam, you can move it. Get your subject out of her chair and capture her walking across the room, or moving back and forth between props. Use the camera in a handheld fashion or, even better, turn it on the tripod to follow the speaker's movement. Even in a small YouTube window, it's okay to have a little action in the shot.

...But Too Much Movement Is Bad

With that said, one sure way to make your video look amateurish is to show off your camera technique by zooming in and out, panning back and forth, and otherwise moving your camera too much. Although some camera movement is good, too much is bad. Don't overuse the zoom and pan; it just makes your video difficult to watch.

This is particularly so when your video plays in a small video window in a web browser, as it is with YouTube. On the Web, extraneous motion is your enemy. Even well-crafted motion can sometimes detract from the message. When creating video for the Web, you want to eliminate all unnecessary motion from both the camera and from the subject.

Worse is high-motion action, such as when capturing sporting events. When each new frame of your video holds substantially different information from the previous frame, you end up unnecessarily increasing the size of your video file. In addition, someone viewing your video on a slow Internet connection might see the action as jerky and disconnected, which is not the effect you want.

For this reason, many video producers try to keep their subjects as stationary as possible in the frame. They also try to keep camera movement to a minimum—no unnecessary zooming, panning, or tilting when a static shot works just as well.

Shoot from Different Angles

Another way to introduce visual interest in your videos is to cut between multiple shots. You might show the presenter speaking directly to the camera and then cut to a short shot of the presenter from the side. This sort of rapid cutting is simply more interesting than a static front-on shot held for three minutes.

You can accomplish this in a number of ways. The easiest way is simply to shoot the video twice: once from the first angle and once from a second angle. You can then intercut shots from both takes in the editing process.

Another approach is to shoot the video only once, but using two cameras, each at a different position. Again, you can intercut shots from both videos during the editing process. The advantage of the two-camera approach is that the two videos are perfectly in sync, which is unlikely using a single-camera approach.

Close-Ups Are Good

While we're talking about using different shots in a video, consider the use of close-ups as one of your alternatives. Let's say you're shooting a product demonstration, which you shoot from an appropriate distance to capture both the presenter and the product. At some point, the presenter presses a particular button on the product, which is difficult to see from several feet away. The solution is to shoot a separate close-up shot of the presenter's finger on the button. You can then cut to this shot at the appropriate point in the video; doing so not only adds visual interest, it better demonstrates that facet of the product.

Don't Center the Subject

When shooting a video for YouTube, it's tempting to place your subject dead center in the video frame. Avoid the temptation.

A much better compositional approach is to use a technique called the *rule of thirds*. With the rule of thirds, you divide the frame into three vertical strips and three horizontal strips, as with a game of tic-tac-toe. You do this by drawing two equidistant vertical lines and two equidistant horizontal lines, as shown in Figure 6.9. This creates nine segments in the frame.

You want to avoid placing the main subject dead center in any of the nine segments. Instead, you want to position the focal point on or close to one of the four points where the vertical and horizontal lines intersect— the small circles in Figure 6.9. Alternatively, for a little more flexibility, you can position the focal point on one of the grid's horizontal or vertical lines. Which intersection point you choose is entirely up to you.

By the way, when you position your subject at one of the rule of thirds intersection points, make sure you have the subject looking into the center of the frame, as shown in Figure 6.10. The alternative is to have your subject staring out of the frame, which is a trifle disconcerting.

FIGURE 6.9

Composing your shot via the rule of thirds.

FIGURE 6.10

Position your subject to the side, looking into the center of the frame.

Shoot to Edit

We get into video editing in Chapter 8, "Editing and Enhancing Your Video." But for better editing, you need to do a little preparation in advance.

The easiest way to make your videos easier to edit is by shooting to edit, which means thinking about your final production before and during the shoot. This lets you capture appropriate shots during the process and keeps the shoot somewhat efficient by shooting only what you need. Not only do you speed up the shooting process, you also can edit much faster when you get to that phase of the operation.

tip

Consider creating a shot list—literally, a list of each shot you make—so you can remember exactly what you captured. A shot list, created in advance, is also helpful when working with a crew, because it lets them know what's coming up.

Use a Teleprompter

Unless your subject is a natural extemporaneous speaker, and few people are, he'll probably speak from some sort of script. That's fine, as long as he can actually read the thing without having to hold a distracting piece of paper in front of him.

The solution to this problem is to use a teleprompter or some semblance of one. A *teleprompter* is simply a device that displays the script, in large type, on a screen mounted next to the camera lens. The speaker can read the script while appearing to look directly into the camera. It's what all the pros and politicians use.

note

Although I use the term teleprompter in a generic fashion, there is an actual device called a TelePrompTer, manufactured by the TelePrompTer Company, which first developed the device in the 1950s.

Although you could purchase an expensive professional teleprompter device, a better semi-pro solution is to turn a notebook computer into an impromptu teleprompter. There are a number of ways to do this, but all involve inputting the speech into a software program that displays the text in large type on the notebook screen. Position the notebook next to or directly below the camera lens, and you're good to go.

If you're looking for a dedicated teleprompter program, consider Prompt! (www.movieclip.biz/prompt.html), which imports text from other programs and converts it into a format ideal for teleprompting. You can also simulate a teleprompter by using speaker notes and Presenter mode in Microsoft PowerPoint.

For a speaker, working with a teleprompter takes a bit of practice; using one for the first time can be tricky. The presenter sees only a few lines of the speech at a time, and there's no way to back up when he passes a particular point. And he's wedded to the speech as written; going off-topic can confuse the teleprompter operator, who must follow along and manually scroll through the speech, line by line. The operator follows the pace of the speech so that the scrolling text follows the speaker as he delivers it. If the speaker slows down, the operator slows down the scroll so that the words scroll slower on screen. If the speaker speeds up, the scrolling speeds up. And if the speaker goes off-topic, the operator doesn't know what to do, which means it's time for another take.

Therefore, it helps to rehearse with the teleprompter ahead of time so that the speaker can get used to reading and speaking at the same time. Fortunately, that's not as hard as it sounds. The key is for the speaker to always speak at his own pace, and trust the teleprompter to follow him. The speaker should never let the scrolling words dictate how fast he talks.

Dress Appropriately

We finish these tips with a word about how the subject of your video should be dressed. The key word is *appropriately* because there's no single right or wrong for every possible type of video.

If your company appeals to young people with a hip and trendy image, don't dress the speaker in a Brooks Brothers suit and tie; khakis and a polo shirt (or jeans and a t-shirt, depending) might be more appropriate. Likewise, you probably don't want to shoot a video for an investment bank using a spokesmodel in a bikini. That wouldn't be appropriate.

You should also consider how the chosen clothing looks onscreen. Avoid clothing with tight or busy patterns; plain shirts are better than striped ones. Don't let the color or brightness of the presenter's clothing conflict with or blend in too much with the shot's background color or pattern. You want the subject to stand out from the background, but not glaringly so.

Here are some additional tips on choosing the most appropriate clothing for your subject:

- Choose clothing that reflects the subject's taste and personality, as well as the image you want to convey for your company or product. Unless you're deliberately striving for a particular effect, avoid clothing that isn't natural for the subject.

- Simplicity is best; go with solid colors or simple patterns. Avoid wild checks, stripes, and busy patterns that tend to draw attention to themselves or that "scream" on camera.

- Clothing should complement the subject's face, not be in conflict with it, which again argues for simplicity.

- The subject should dress comfortably, especially if it's going to be a long shooting session. Although a suit and tie are *de rigueur* for many corporate videos, more casual videos might call for turtlenecks, V-necks, open-collared shirts, and sweaters.

- For fancier videos, it's a good idea for the subject to have at least one change of clothes. This provides some flexibility and offers more choices when it comes to choosing the final shot.

- Women should generally avoid showing bare arms; it's better to wear long-sleeved shirts and blouses instead. (And the no-bare-arms rule goes double for men!)

- Similarly, women in full-length shots should almost always wear slacks, a long skirt, or dark stockings. It's not a good idea to show a lot of skin that draws attention away from the subject's face.

- In terms of color, darker colors are generally better than lighter ones. The best colors are medium shades of blue, green, rust, and burgundy.

- White, yellow, pink, and similar colors tend to overpower the subject's face and make her look pale.

- You should avoid bright reds and oranges. They draw attention away from the subject's face and from any product he's demonstrating!

But these are just general guidelines, not hard and fast rules. Go for what works best in your particular shot. Remember to envision the shot as it will look in YouTube's small 320×240 resolution video window!

The Big Picture

For most small and medium-sized businesses, and even many large ones, shooting semi-pro videos is the best way to create content for YouTube. All you need is a low-cost consumer camcorder and a few accessories, and you can create all different types of videos with surprisingly professional results. In fact, most of the videos featured in the profile sections of this book came about in this fashion, to remarkable effect.

What do you need to create a professional-looking video on a limited budget? Not much: just a camcorder, a tripod, and perhaps some sort of auxiliary lighting and external microphone. Of course, you also need a computer and video-editing software to edit the videos you shoot. But that's not a large investment, and you can achieve impressive results with this approach. It's certainly preferable to investing in expensive professional productions—at least in the early stages of your YouTube experience. ■

7

Shooting Professional Videos

Most YouTube videos, even those produced by businesses, come from standard consumer-grade equipment in the comfort of someone's living room, office, or conference room. Few YouTubers, even businesses, go to the trouble and expense of enlisting professional video makers to produce their videos; the expense is too great and the return too small.

But with that said, there might be times when you want to enlist a professional video production company to create a video for your business. The production company might send a cameraman and crew to your offices, or you might travel to a sound stage or studio to shoot the video there. In either instance, the result is a much better looking (and sounding) video than you can create on your own, with a lot more editing and special effects options.

Of course, you pay for higher-quality results. A professionally produced video could cost $5,000 to $50,000 or even more, depending on the length and complexity of the shoot and the amount of editing necessary to create the final cut. But if the video presents the image you want to portray on YouTube, it might be the only way to go.

Why Create a Professional Video for YouTube?

When the vast majority of YouTube videos come from consumer camcorders or webcams, why go to the expense of creating an expensive professionally produced video? There are some good reasons to do so, and some equally good reasons not to.

Advantages of Professional Videos

One of the main reasons to produce a professional video is that it looks professional. Let's face it: The average YouTube video looks amateurish, which is what you expect when amateurs are doing the shooting using consumer-grade equipment. That's fine for many businesses, but if you're in charge of marketing for a large multinational corporation, you might not want your YouTube presence to look as if your cousin Jim did the filming in his basement.

This is why you see companies such as Intuit, Nike, and Smirnoff spending big bucks to create videos for their YouTube channels. Their videos might lack the immediacy of webcam-produced video blogs, but they pack the much more powerful punch that their brands demand. In fact, many of their YouTube videos resemble traditional commercials—or in many cases, extended versions of commercials.

tip

On YouTube, you're not limited to 30-second spots, as you are with traditional broadcast commercials. You can take advantage of the longer length to present a more-detailed message.

So, if you represent a big company with a big message and a big budget, going with a professionally produced video makes a lot of sense. In effect, this is what your customers expect; anything less would invite cognitive dissonance into your brand message.

Disadvantages of Professional Videos

Of course, the primary disadvantage of going the professional route is that YouTube users might reject your message as being too commercial. It's a double-edged sword; you have a commercial message to impart, but the YouTube community is resolutely anticommercial in nature. Unless your video is extremely entertaining or equally informative, you could end up receiving more negative comments than positive ones.

In addition, a pro-quality video might be overkill for YouTube, especially when it comes to video quality and production values. Your video, no matter how much money you spend on it, is still seen in the same 320×240 video window as basement-quality webcam videos. The typical

YouTube viewer, watching in his web browser, might not even see the better lighting, quality makeup, and appealing backdrops. A lot of money can get lost in the resolution.

> **note**
>
> A few years ago, I hosted a series of videos for a major website (not YouTube). The website spent some big bucks to rent a studio, hire a crew, and execute the shoot—money that definitely wasn't seen onscreen. At one point, the wardrobe person asked what kind of shoes I'd be wearing—even though the shot was from the waist up! And even if it were a full-length shot, no one could see what was on my feet in a 320×240 video window. As I said, it was a lot of money lost on a low-resolution video.

Money is the real killer for a lot of businesses. Expect to pay in the range of $1,000 to $3,000 per minute of finished video. In most instances, you're looking at a minimum of $5,000 for a two- or three-minute video, with big shoots (requiring lots of studio time and personnel) costing three or four times that much. It's not cheap.

Bottom line, a professional video costs a lot more money than one you create yourself. Ask yourself whether you'll see the results of that expense. In addition, ask yourself whether your target audience in the YouTube community responds well to this type of video.

What Makes a Professional Video Professional

To the untrained eye, there might be little difference between a well-done semi-pro video and a professionally produced video. But professionals can tell the difference; it's a matter of trained professionals using quality equipment to produce superior results.

Shooting can be either on location (typically in your offices) or in a video production studio. Both have their advantages.

Shooting in the Studio

Shooting in the studio has the advantage of more equipment and props on hand. This is especially important in lighting and sound, which can be better controlled in a studio environment.

When you first visit the studio, its size is likely to impress you. Most production studios are built around large sound stages, big spaces in which all manner of props and backdrops are used. For example, you might see some sort of curved seamless background, or perhaps a large curtain or roll of seamless background paper, in front of which the subject stands. This background is typically a neutral color; technicians shine colored lights on the background if a colored background is necessary.

You'll see one or more rows of spotlights on the ceiling, as well as various auxiliary lights mounted on stands. You'll also see various baffles, diffusers, and reflectors—all to better direct the right lighting to the right spots in the frame.

You'll shoot the video in front of the chosen background, lit by the appropriate studio lights. One or more DV or Betacam cameras, mounted on tripods or tracks (for moving shoots), typically do the shooting. If more than one camera is used, they're synchronized via time code to make for easier editing between shots.

Sound can be recorded in a number of different ways. Some studios prefer to mic each subject individually, typically with a wireless lavaliere microphone. Other studios prefer the old-school approach, using a boom microphone held over the heads of the subjects, just out of camera range. In both cases, a separate soundman is typically responsible for getting the best possible sound.

If the subject is reading from a script, and he probably is, you'll find a teleprompter mounted on top of each camera. The script for the video is entered into the teleprompter system via keyboard, and the teleprompter operator controls the scrolling speed of the script.

In addition to the camera operators, soundmen, and teleprompter operator, the crew might also include one or more lighting specialists, makeup and wardrobe people, various assistants and gofers, and, of course, a director. For a typical shoot, this means a crew of anywhere from a half-dozen to a dozen people—a lot more people than are typically involved with a semi-pro video.

Figure 7.1 shows how this all looks in a real-world setting. This photograph shows your humble author in a (non-YouTube) video shoot in a professional studio. I'm standing in front of a curved seamless background, surrounded by various lights, diffusers, and baffles. The camera is mounted on a four-wheeled trolley that travels on a set of train-type tracks; one person pushes the trolley for moving shots. It's very bright, and very busy, and very exciting, especially if it's your first time in the studio. In fact, it's so busy that it's sometimes hard to keep your concentration!

FIGURE 7.1

A video shoot in a professional studio—look at all that equipment!

Shooting in the Field

As you can see, shooting in the studio is a big production with a correspondingly big expense. A better approach, for some videos, is to use a remote production crew to shoot in the field—that is, at your location, rather than in the studio. A location shoot is typically less involved and often less expensive than renting a production studio with full crew.

A location shoot can be as simple as one guy with a camera. Of course, the camera is a pro-grade DV or Betacam model, and the cameraman carries a set of portable lights and a wireless lavaliere microphone. He mics the subject, sets up and aims the lights, mounts the camera on a tripod, and starts shooting.

note

In some instances, a mobile camera operator might be accompanied by an assistant to help set up the equipment.

The results of a location shoot, depending on the environment, can be as professional as that created in a studio. In most instances, however, a remote shoot has a slightly different look and feel, somewhat akin to that of a remote TV news report—more immediate, less polished.

Even though a location shoot uses less equipment and a smaller crew, it still can be more involved than a typical semi-pro shoot. Expect the camera operator to be very demanding, being critical about shadows, background noise, and slips of the tongue; multiple takes are obligatory. Just because you're shooting on location doesn't mean that standards are relaxed.

---

tip

One of the chief advantages of a location shoot is that you don't have to take your company's personnel out of the office for an entire day. The video crew arrives, sets up their stuff, and then calls in the "talent" for the shoot. This can be an important factor, especially when your "talent" consists of busy upper management.

Preparing for a Professional Video Shoot

If you're in charge of creating a professional video, you need to do a few things to prepare your "talent" for the shoot. It isn't as simple as showing up and smiling; there's a lot of upfront work necessary before the cameras start rolling.

---

note

In industry parlance, the *talent* is the person who appears on camera.

Make Friends with Makeup

This is a big deal, especially for guys. One of the primary reasons that professionals look so good onscreen is because they wear the right makeup. Makeup artists make big bucks in Hollywood and New York; the right makeup can make normal people look like stars, whereas the wrong makeup (or no makeup at all) can make even the most beautiful, blemish-free people look average on camera.

So, even if your talent is nonprofessional, you still have to work through the makeup angle. If your stars want to look good on camera, they have to wear the proper makeup. And make sure your people know that this applies not just to women, but also to any males in front of the camera—it's an important issue.

One problem in producing your own videos is that you probably don't know beans about makeup. This is another area where a pro video shoot differs from an amateur shoot; when you hire a video production firm, a makeup person should be included as part of the deal. The makeup should be tonal to get rid of glare on the face; if the subject's hands are visible in the video, tone them, too.

Learn Your Shooting Angles

You've heard Hollywood types tell photographers to shoot them only from their good side. That might sound vain, and probably is, but there's also a bit of truth to it. Most people look better when shot from one side than the other. A skilled cameraman or director knows this and positions the camera accordingly.

In addition, you don't always want to face the camera head-on. A better shot often results from the subject's body turned to the left or right of the camera, with the head turned to face the camera. This slight body angle is more visually interesting and avoids a boring "talking head" appearance.

Wait for the Lighting

One of the things you have to get used to on a professional video shoot is the waiting; there's a lot of it. You might spend a full eight-hour day just to get three minutes of finished video. Although some of that time comes from multiple takes (the talent almost never gets it perfect in one shot), much of the time is spent waiting for the technicians to get the lighting right.

Lighting is important in a professional video. That's why they use more than just one light in the studio; there's typically a bank of lights above the stage and even more sitting around the side on stands. The director wants to light the subject (and every other important item in the shot) as flatteringly as possible, which takes time. One light aimed here, another aimed there, maybe a diffuser added in front of this one and a reflector to the side of that one—it's all very involved.

Lighting experts talk about direct lighting and indirect lighting, fill lights and bounce lights, main lights and hair lights. You don't have to know what all these things are—only that they're all important and take time to get in just the right position. The subject of a video has to be prepared to stand in one spot for long periods, being as patient as possible while technicians adjust all the various lights and accessories. Then, and only then, can the shoot proceed.

Prepare for Multiple Takes

Few professional videos happen in a single take. Most subjects require multiple takes to get one perfect reading, and even then the director might want yet another take as a safety. In addition, it's likely that the video consists of several different shots, intercut in the editing room. That probably involves delivering the same reading multiple times, with the camera moved to a different angle for each shot. Editors intercut the subsidiary shots into the master shot for more visual variety.

The key here is for the talent to deliver his or her lines not just perfectly, but identically across multiple takes. That's why most directors prefer the talent to read from a teleprompter script, rather than speaking extemporaneously. If the talent is improvising on each take, it makes it next to impossible to match shots from multiple takes into a cohesive whole. The best on-air talent nails a perfect and consistent reading take after take after mother-lovin' take.

If this sounds boring, it is; it's also a special skill that not everyone has. Those infomercial hosts and newsreaders might not have a spontaneous cell in their brains, but they do have the ability to speak clearly and consistently from a script. It's harder than you think.

The Big Picture

Most businesses don't go to the effort and expense of producing professional-quality videos for YouTube, and for good reason. Not only are professional videos considerably more expensive than the semi-pro type you can shoot on your own, but they're also often too slick for the savvy YouTube audience. Tread carefully into these waters.

If you choose to go the professional route, go into it with your eyes wide open. Expect to spend a minimum of $5,000 or so and to spend a full day in the studio shooting—a little less in terms of both money and time if you shoot on location in your own offices. And there's a lot of prep work involved in writing a script, arranging makeup, and the like. It's a fun experience, but it is an experience. Make sure everyone involved is properly prepared. ■

8

Editing and Enhancing Your Videos

Few videos are YouTube-ready out of the box, even those produced by professionals. No, you probably want to cut out the boring parts, trim the whole thing down to no more than 10 minutes (less is probably better), and convert the video to a YouTube-friendly 320×240 MPEG-4 file. You might even want to add titles, onscreen graphics, scene transitions, and other special effects.

Does that sound like a lot of work? It doesn't have to be—assuming that you have a well-powered personal computer and the right video-editing software.

Choosing a Video-Editing Program

In the not-so-distant past, if you wanted to edit a video, you had to use an expensive dedicated video-editing console, such as the ones found in local and network television studios. Not so today—any moderately powered personal computer, equipped with the right software, does the job quite nicely and at a much lower cost. Today's video-editing software lets you cut and rearrange scenes, add fancy transitions between scenes, add titles (and subtitles), and even add your own music soundtrack. The results are amazing!

There are four tiers of video-editing programs available, easily identifiable by price. The first-tier programs are free, the second-tier programs cost around $100, the third-tier programs run between $200 and $600, and the top tier costs $800 or more. We examine each tier separately.

Tier One: Free Programs

The first tier of video-editing programs is one of the most popular—because the software is free! In reality, these programs come bundled with your computer's operating system, which means there's one version for Windows and another for the Mac.

For the typical YouTube video producer, these programs do a good job. They include basic editing features, as well as scene transitions, titles, and other similar capabilities. They're not quite as high powered or flexible as the higher-priced programs, but how much power and flexibility do you need when creating videos for YouTube?

---

note

You might also have received a video-editing program when you purchased a camcorder. Some manufacturers offer their own video-editing programs or "lite" versions of other popular programs.

Windows Movie Maker

If your computer is running either Windows XP or Windows Vista, you have a full-featured video-editing program already installed on your PC. That program is Windows Movie Maker, and although it's not as sophisticated as some of the other video-editing programs, it includes all the features you need to do basic home video editing.

Like more expensive programs, Windows Movie Maker enables you to import videos in a variety of formats, edit your videos on a scene-by-scene basis, and add elements such as scene transitions, static or animated titles and credits, secondary audio tracks, and other special effects. You can save your video in Windows Media and AVI formats or burn it directly to DVD.

As shown in Figure 8.1, you edit in either a Storyboard or Timeline view. In Storyboard view, the project appears as a filmstrip, with each scene as a separate element on the strip; use this view to add transitions between scenes or to apply special effects to specific scenes. In Timeline view, you can edit the video on a second-by-second basis and stretch elements to fill a specific timeslot.

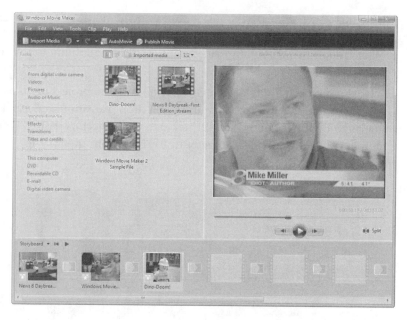

FIGURE 8.1

Windows Movie Maker—a free video editor ideal for YouTube use.

To create a video project, simply drag individual clips (scenes) onto the storyboard or timeline. You apply transitions and special effects in the same way: by dragging and dropping them onto the desired scene. Or if you like, you can use the program's AutoMovie option to apply predefined styles to your video for quick project creation.

In short, Windows Movie Maker is an easy-to-use, completely free program and is available to anyone running Windows XP or Vista. It's an ideal solution for those with modest editing needs—like most YouTube content creators.

Apple iMovie

Windows Movie Maker is exclusively for Windows users, but if you're a Macintosh user, you have a similar preinstalled solution. Apple includes its iLife software with all Macs, and the iLife suite includes the iMovie video-editing program. Like Windows Movie Maker, iMovie is a surprisingly full-featured video-editing program, quite easy to use, and completely free.

iMovie includes a variety of useful features, including transitions, titles, and special effects. Also useful are the powerful color correction tools, a tool for cropping and zooming video clips, and the capability to rotate videos.

To create a project, simply drag a clip (scene) into the project area, as shown in Figure 8.2. You can then drag and drop transitions, effects, titles, and even an optional audio soundtrack into the project as desired. You can upload completed videos directly to YouTube from the iMovie interface.

FIGURE 8.2
iMovie—Apple's free video-editing program.

note

For a short time, YouTube offered its own free online video-editing program, dubbed YouTube Remixer. The program proved to be a disappointment, however, and YouTube subsequently took it off the site.

Tier Two: Inexpensive Programs

Windows Movie Maker and iMovie are ideal for many YouTube video creators, but they're not the most-sophisticated programs around. (What do you expect at no charge?) If you find yourself wanting more or different special effects, or greater control over your video editing, it's time to invest in a freestanding video-editing program.

This second tier of video-editing programs consists of a multitude of relatively inexpensive programs. Prices on these programs run from about $50 to $150—certainly affordable for most businesses.

Adobe Premiere Elements

Adobe is the premier producer of digital photography and video-editing programs, and the company's main video-editing product is Adobe Premiere. The company makes two versions of Premiere: the full-featured Premiere Studio CS, which we discuss later in this chapter, and the more affordably priced Premiere Elements, which is a Windows-only program.

Premiere Elements got its name because it includes key elements from the more expensive Premiere Studio CS product. It's the product of choice for many amateur video makers, priced at just $99.99. You can learn more about the program at www.adobe.com/products/premiereel/.

The latest version (4) of Premiere Elements, shown in Figure 8.3, includes a sleek interface that includes a video preview window, a task panel that includes various content and effects controls, and a timeline/sceneline along the bottom. Different tabs enable you to perform different types of editing (Media, Themes, Effects, Transitions, and Titles), most of which occurs via convenient drag-and-drop functionality. Predesigned themes let you jump-start the video-editing process.

FIGURE 8.3

Adobe Premiere Elements—an affordable video-editing solution.

You can create multiple video and audio tracks for your video. This lets you easily transition from one clip to another or mix background music and sound effects into your video. Naturally, the program includes a variety of animated titles and transitions. The program features automatic formatting and uploading for YouTube.

ArcSoft ShowBiz DVD

ShowBiz DVD from ArcSoft is an easy-to-use program that includes video editing and DVD creation. It's a Windows-only program and is available from www.arcsoft.com/en/products/showbiz/ for $99.99.

The video-editing part of the program features the obligatory Storyboard view for arranging various video clips, as well as a more advanced Timeline view that gives you more control over your clips, audio tracks, transitions, and special effects. You can also use the program to create photo slideshow videos.

CyberLink PowerDirector

CyberLink's PowerDirector is another easy-to-use video-editing/DVD creation program. It's a Windows-only program and is available from www.cyberlink.com/ for $89.95.

Like most of these programs, PowerDirector provides a selection of transitions, titles, and special effects. You also get some neat enhancement tools to fix and improve less than perfect videos. It imports high definition video and publishes videos direct to YouTube.

MoviePlus

MoviePlus offers digital video editing and DVD creation. It's a Windows-only program, and is available from www.serif.com/movieplus/movieplus5/ for $79.99.

The program's feature set is similar to other competing programs. It imports high definition video and includes a variety of transitions and special effects; it also lets you easily create photo slideshow videos.

Nero Ultra Edition

Nero Ultra Edition is actually a suite of digital multimedia-editing tools. In addition to video editing, you get photo editing, audio editing, and similar functionality. The program also offers CD and DVD burning and sells for $99.99 from www.nero.com. As with most of the other low price programs, it's for Windows only.

For the video-editing part of the suite, Nero offers a user-friendly interface, supports high definition video, and provides easy exporting and uploading to YouTube. It can also save videos to DVD or to an iPod or PSP (PlayStation Portable).

Pinnacle Studio

Pinnacle offers three different versions of its Pinnacle Studio video-editing program: Pinnacle Studio ($49.99), Pinnacle Studio Plus ($99.99), and Pinnacle Studio Ultimate ($129.99). All three versions of this Windows-only program enable you to combine video clips with still photos and MP3 audio tracks and then add your own transitions and effects. The Plus version, shown in Figure 8.4, adds HD editing, whereas the Ultimate version adds a full complement of professional audio- and video-editing tools. More information is available at www.pinnaclesys.com/.

FIGURE 8.4

Pinnacle Studio—a video-editing program chock-full of special effects, such as picture-in-picture.

The Ultimate version might be the best choice for some users because it includes SoundSoap audio-cleaning tools for reducing noise on soundtracks, and video panning and scanning effects via the StageTool MovingPicture add-in. More special effects are available via the Vitascene add-in, which lets you add sparkle effects, a binocular mask, a soft white vignette, and old-film effects. You can even use a chroma key greenscreen backdrop for professional behind-the-subject effects.

tip

Even though Pinnacle Studio Ultimate costs a little more than the other second-tier programs, the quality and quantity of the special effects offered make it the program of choice for many budget-conscious video makers.

Roxio VideoWave

Roxio VideoWave is one of the lowest priced second-tier video-editing programs. Priced at just $49.99, it offers easy-to-use operation and basic editing and effects. More information on this Windows-only program is available at www.roxio.com/.

Like many of these programs, VideoWave is a combination video editor and CD/DVD creator. It features easy importing of camcorder video, scene- and timeline-based editing, and a CineMagic feature that automates the addition of transitions and other special effects. It also supports high definition video and Dolby Digital sound.

Sony Vegas Movie Studio

Sony's Vegas Movie Studio is a surprisingly powerful video-editing program. Priced at $74.95, you can purchase this Windows-only software at www.sonycreativesoftware.com/products/vegasfamily.asp.

note

Vegas Movie Studio is also available in a $114.95 Platinum Edition that adds high definition video (HDV) capability, 5.1-channel surround sound, color correction tools, and direct export to the PSP/iPod video format.

Vegas Movie Studio is a combination video editor and DVD-authoring program. The video-editing component includes more than 185 professional transitions and nearly 300 customizable special effects—including a greenscreen feature and something called the "Ken Burns Effect," which makes for more interesting photo slideshow videos. Editing is via a familiar drag-and-drop interface.

note

Ken Burns is the PBS documentary filmmaker known for his panning and scanning and zooming of archival photographs.

Ulead VideoStudio

Another popular video-editing/DVD authoring program is Ulead VideoStudio. This Windows-only program is available from www.ulead.com/vs/ for $89.99.

VideoStudio features three different ways to create a video. The DV-to-DVD Wizard burns your camcorder's video directly to DVD (not great for YouTube); the Movie Wizard helps to automate the video creation process; and the VideoStudio Editor gives you complete control over your video's editing. You get useful auto color and tone filters, as well as DeBlock and DeSnow filters to clean up the recorded video.

> **note**
>
> Ulead VideoStudio is also available in a $129.99 Plus version, which adds support for high definition video, Dolby Digital 5.1 surround sound, and the iPod/PSP H.264 video format, as well as multiple overlay tracks for picture-in-picture and montage effects.

Tier Three: Mid-Range Programs

Most of the second-tier programs offer similar features and similar functionality; they all work in pretty much the same fashion, using a combination of clip or scene views and timeline views. If you want more powerful editing and fancier special effects, you have to move up to the third tier of programs, those priced from $200 to $500 or so. There are three programs in this class: Apple Final Cut Express, Sony Vegas Pro, and Ulead MediaStudio Pro.

Apple Final Cut Express

Let's start by discussing Apple's Final Cut Express. This is a slightly stripped down version of the company's full-featured Final Cut Pro software and a big step up from the free iMovie program. It's available for $199 from www.apple.com/finalcutexpress/. As you might suspect, this is a Mac-only program.

As you can see in Figure 8.5, Final Cut Express offers an assortment of sophisticated transitions, filters, and effects, including dynamic animated text. You can also use multiple audio tracks, utilize automatic audio levels, and employ various advanced audio filters.

FIGURE 8.5

Final Cut Express—big-time video editing at a small-time price.

The program works with both standard and high-resolution video from any digital camcorder. You can mix and match video formats in the program's timeline, using traditional drag-and-drop editing. You have a comprehensive set of editing options, including insert, overwrite, fit-to-fill, and such; you can fine-tune your edits with a variety of trim options, such as ripple, roll, slip, slide, extend, and shorten. Final Cut Pro even lets you create professional-quality *L cuts*, where the audio and video start at different times.

Sony Vegas Pro

A tad more on the expensive side, Sony's Vegas Pro is actually a suite of related products. For $549.95, you get the Vegas video editor, the DVD Architect DVD-authoring program, and Dolby Digital (AC-3)–encoding software. More information on this Windows-only solution is available at www.sonycreativesoftware.com/products/vegasfamily.asp.

Vegas Pro's editing tools for both standard and high definition video use both mouse and keyboard trimming. You get ProType Titling technology, tools to edit multicamera shoots, auto-frame quantization, and other pro-level tools. On the audio front, Vegas Pro lets you use unlimited audio tracks with punch-in recording, 5.1-channel surround mixing, and real-time automation for various audio effects, including equalization (EQ), reverb, delay, and more. As you can see in Figure 8.6, all these tools are combined in a busy but easily navigable interface—just what you'd expect from a semi-pro level program like this.

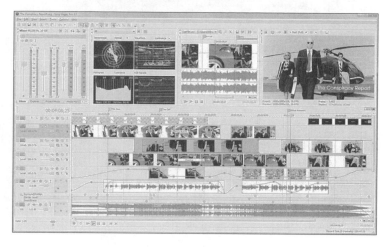

FIGURE 8.6

Vegas Pro—a sophisticated interface for a powerful video-editing program.

This is a powerful program, offering many of the professional editing functions and effects as found on the top-tier programs, but at a slightly lower price.

Ulead MediaStudio Pro

Our final semi-pro video-editing program is Ulead MediaStudio Pro, a Windows-only program that sells for $399.99 from www.ulead.com/msp/. As you can see in Figure 8.7, the program features a traditional timeline-editing mode, but with a separate Effects Manager for adding transitions and other special effects. The program is a good compromise between price and performance if you're on a budget.

MediaStudio Pro edits both standard and high definition video with Dolby Digital 5.1-channel sound. It includes a "smart compositor" that lets you easily create professional-quality sequences and segues, with premade masks, frames, and moving paths. You can choose from a variety of pre-designed themes, which helps to speed up the production task. The editing functions include real-time audio mixing, two types of color correction, and a dynamic title tool.

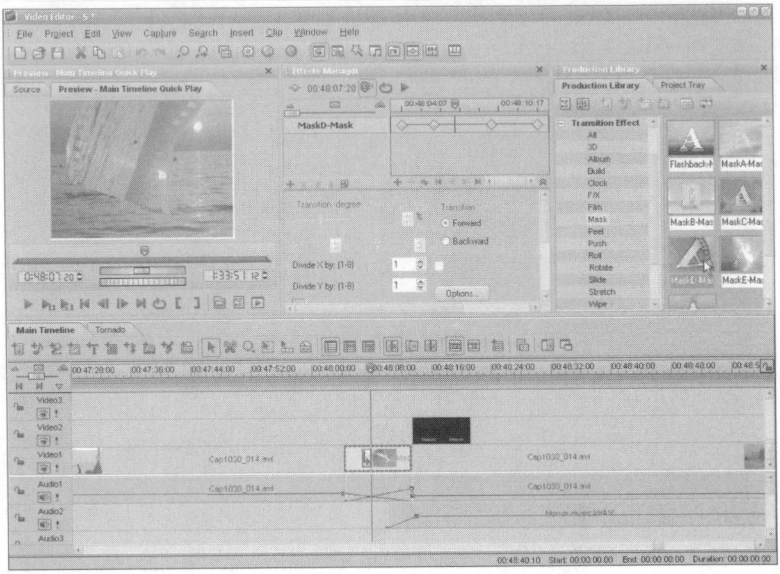

FIGURE 8.7
Ulead MediaStudio Pro—a semi-pro video-editing solution.

Tier Four: High-End Programs

If you want true professional-quality editing and effects, and money is no object, these final two programs are worth considering. Both Adobe Premiere Pro CS3 and Apple Final Cut Studio are true pro-level video-editing programs, with much more sophisticated features and functionality than the other programs previously discussed—including multi-track editing, advanced audio editing, and a greater number of more sophisticated titles, transitions, and special effects.

Adobe Premiere Pro CS

For many video creators, the ultimate video-editing suite is Adobe Premiere Pro CS. At $799, the program isn't cheap; for the price, however, you get a variety of different software programs that help you create truly professional videos. (More information is available at www.adobe.com/products/premiere/; the program is available in both Windows and Mac versions.)

Figure 8.8 gives you a flavor of what Adobe Premiere Pro CS offers. The interface changes a bit depending on what type of editing you're doing at the time, but you have the expected timeline editor, video window, and a bevy of available editing, audio, and video effects.

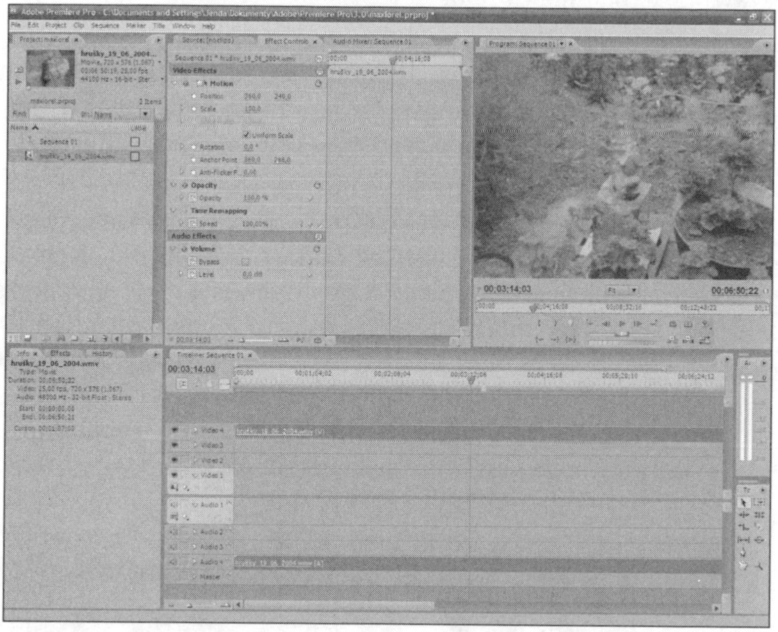

FIGURE 8.8

Adobe Premiere Pro CS—a pro-level video-editing suite.

Adobe Premiere Pro CS works seamlessly with professional video equipment from Panasonic and Sony, with native editing for both companies' proprietary media formats. You can generate a variety of high-quality video effects, including slow motion and other time-remapping effects. Also available are professional-caliber color correction, lighting effects, audio filters, and more. The program also makes it easy to edit footage from multicamera shoots.

Naturally, Premiere Pro works with both standard and high definition video. It integrates seamlessly with other Adobe applications, including Photoshop and After Effects.

Apple Final Cut Studio

Adobe's chief competitor in the high-end video-editing space is Apple Final Cut Studio, a Mac-only suite that retails for $1,299. The suite includes the Final Cut Pro video editor, along with Color (professional color grading), Motion (3D motion graphics), Soundtrack Pro (audio post production), Compressor (encoding for different video formats), and DVD Studio Pro (DVD authoring). You can find more information at www.apple.com/finalcutstudio/.

Apple claims more than one million users of its Final Cut software; it's definitely the first choice of professional video editors worldwide. Final Cut Studio works with virtually any video format, including high-definition and professional formats. You can easily combine clips of different formats on the program's timeline.

As you can see in Figure 8.9, Final Cut Studio offers a wide variety of sophisticated video special effects—including the ability to create 3D multiplane environments. Even better than all the cool transitions and special effects is the Color component, which enables you to create a consistent look and feel for shots from different sources; this elevates the quality of any production to a truly professional level. Also useful in this regard is the program's SmoothCam feature that automatically stabilizes shaky shots while preserving the original camera moves.

FIGURE 8.9
Apple Final Cut Studio—complete with sophisticated 3D video effects.

Using a Video-Editing Program

Whether you use a free video-editing program or one that costs $1,000 or more, you use the program to do pretty much the same tasks: edit together multiple scenes, add titles and transitions before and between scenes, and apply any desired special effects. If the program allows it, you can also choose to clean up your audio and video, using various color correction and noise reduction tools.

How do you perform these essential tasks? Obviously, the specific steps vary from program to program, but the general approach remains the same. Read on to learn more.

note

For the examples in this section, we use Windows Movie Maker, the free video-editing program included with both Windows XP and Windows Vista. Similar features are available in other programs and work in similar ways.

Editing Together Different Shots

Unless you shot your video in a single continuous take, you probably have multiple takes and shots to work with. To create an interesting video, you need to edit these various clips together into a cohesive whole so that the video flows from shot to shot and scene to scene.

In most video-editing programs, you have the ability to work in some sort of clip view. This involves dragging and dropping individual clips onto the program's storyboard. As you can see in Figure 8.10, the storyboard is a filmstrip-type area in the interface. You can easily change the order of clips on the filmstrip and delete clips that you don't want in the final video. Just keep rearranging clips until your video is in the order that you want.

FIGURE 8.10

Arrange multiple video clips into a single storyboard.

The key to effective editing is to tell a cohesive story. Don't jump around from topic to topic; more importantly, don't jump around temporally. Tell a linear story from start to finish; don't make the viewer work hard to figure out what's going on. Make sure one shot leads logically and directly to the next without any glaring gaps. If you're not sure whether the scene order works, just watch the video from start to finish—if you can't follow the threads, re-edit!

Inserting Transitions Between Scenes

There are numerous ways to move from one clip or shot to another within a video. The most direct approach is to use a *jump cut* where one scene abruptly cuts to the next, with no fancy transition. Although this can sometimes be jarring, it's a commonly used technique.

Another approach is to ease the flow from scene to scene by using a transition of some sort. This might be a fade, a wipe, or something fancier, such as some sort of revolving or rotating effect. The key is to match the transition with the onscreen action. For example, if one scene ends with the subject punching forward into the camera, cutting to the next scene via some sort of shatter or "breaking glass" transition might work well.

caution

Avoid overusing some of the fancier transitions. The more animated the transition, the more attention it draws to itself—and away from the video itself.

In most programs, you add a transition by dragging the icon for that transition onto either a clip in the storyboard or a specific area between clips. Figure 8.11 shows just some of the transitions available in the Windows Movie Maker program.

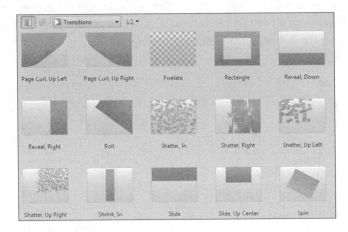

FIGURE 8.11

Add transition effects between video clips.

When deciding what transitions to use, less is more. That is, fancy transitions tend to draw attention to themselves—kind of like, "Hey! Look at this gee-whiz transition effect!" So, it's best to avoid spins and whirls and shatters and the like. Simple old school transitions, such as fades, dissolves, and iris ins/outs are best, even if you think they're a tad boring. Ultimately, the transition should go unnoticed by the viewer; what's important is moving seamlessly from one scene to the next.

In addition, know that transitions are less effective in the small YouTube video window, solely due to the size of the thing. Fancy transitions can also "choke" video playback, especially for viewers with slower Internet connections. So, especially where YouTube is concerned, simpler transitions are definitely better.

Inserting Titles and Credits

Just as important as scene transitions are the titles and credits you add before and after the main body of your video. The main title, like the one shown in Figure 8.12, introduces the video to YouTube viewers. The credits provide more information, direct the viewer to your website, and provide proper credit to the individuals that worked to create the video.

FIGURE 8.12

Insert a title sequence before the start of your main video.

Most video-editing programs let you choose from various styles of titles and credits. You can choose the font type, size, and color; the background pattern or color; and the transition effect between the title and the main video. In most instances, this is as easy as typing your text into the program and then selecting the desired style or theme.

Creating Other Onscreen Graphics

Titles and credits don't have to be the only onscreen text in your video. You can also superimpose other text and graphics on your picture, anywhere in the course of the video.

For example, Figure 8.13 shows a subtitle added to a piece of video. In this instance, it identifies the speaker (your humble author). You can typically choose from a number of different colors, themes, and effects for these onscreen graphics.

FIGURE 8.13
Add onscreen graphics to identify what's happening onscreen.

Adding Background Music

Many video-editing programs let you enhance the video you shoot with background music. This is typically added as a separate track to the program's timeline or storyboard, as shown in Figure 8.14; just drag and drop the chosen music file (typically in MP3 format) into the proper position. You can then adjust the sound level of the music track to best blend the background music with the foreground speaking.

FIGURE 8.14
Add background music via a separate audio track in the timeline.

When choosing background music, make sure the music you choose is the right length for the accompanying video—you don't want the music to end before the video or scene is over. The background music should complement the onscreen action, not overpower it in terms of volume level, lyrical content, and beat/feel. For example, you don't want to accompany an emotional confessional video with an up-tempo hip-hop beat. Select carefully and sympathetically and remember, that it's the main content that matters, not the music in the background.

caution

Make sure you have permission to use the chosen background music. Most music you hear on the radio or CD has a copyright, and you cannot use it for any purpose without express permission. For this reason, you might want to use the public domain music supplied with many video-editing programs—no copyright problems!

Getting Creative with Other Special Effects

Most video-editing programs let you add a plethora of other special effects. For example, you might be able to decolorize the entire video, add an old-timey sepia tone effect, or make the video look like well-worn film stock. Some programs even let you play around with the video's time perspective by speeding up the video or slowing it down into slow motion.

tip

For most business-oriented videos, you want to keep it simple—keep the fancy special effects to a minimum.

You typically add special effects one scene at a time. In most programs, that means dragging and dropping a special effects icon onto a specific clip in the program's storyboard or timeline. The program adds the effect to that clip as it processes the video. To apply the same effect to multiple clips, just do more dragging and dropping.

Although some special effects can be useful in special situations, most business videos need a straight-ahead approach that argues against the more creative of these effects. Remember, you want the viewer to pay attention to your video's content and not to the way it looks or the special effects you use. Use special effects minimally to keep them special.

Converting and Saving Video Files

When you finish all your editing and apply all your transitions and special effects, it's time to save your work. In most video-editing programs, this is a two-step process: First you save the project, and then you process or publish the final video. This second step involves a lot of computer processing because it compiles all the clips and effects you select into a single video file.

When compiling your final video, save it as an AVI or a MPG file, at 640×480 resolution, and with MP3 audio. These specs ensure the best quality playback on the YouTube site—after YouTube converts your file to its own Flash format, of course.

note

Videos all converted and edited? Learn how to upload your videos in Chapter 9, "Uploading Your Videos to YouTube."

The Big Picture

Unless you want the raw look and feel of an unedited webcam video, you need to do some editing of the video you shoot with your camcorder or webcam. This necessitates the use of a video-editing program on a personal computer.

Although you can use a free program such as Windows Movie Maker or Apple iMovie, or a professional program such as Adobe Premiere Pro CS3 or Apple Final Cut Studio, most video creators get the best results from a low-cost program such as Adobe Premiere Elements or Ulead VideoStudio. These programs let you do sophisticated editing and add pro-level special effects and transitions; the results are close to what you see on local newscasts and network television programs. The key is to pick a program that offers the features you need, with an easy-to-use interface, and then to learn all the ins and outs of that program.

Just because a video-editing program can do all sorts of fancy stuff doesn't mean that you need to use every one of the program's bells and whistles. Most videos benefit from minimal editing; too many special effects draw attention to themselves. The key is to edit your video to tell a logical, straightforward story, using available effects to move the story forward rather than to impress the viewer with how sophisticated you are. ∎

YouTube BUSINESS PROFILE

Profile: Charles Smith Pottery

How to sell creative arts and crafts on YouTube? The answer, as noted potter Charles Smith discovered, is to offer viewers educational and informational viewing that inspires sales.

Company Profile

    Company: Charles Smith Pottery

    Product: Pottery

    YouTube channel: www.youtube.com/user/smithpots

    Website: www.smith-pots.com

About Charles Smith and His Pottery

Charles Smith is one of the premiere African-American artists in the United States. He works with stoneware, decorating each piece using a carved-and-sgraffito technique. His style derives from realistic and Art Nouveau forms mixed and interspersed with abstract animal imagery.

Artist Charles Smith.

Smith studied his art at Jackson State University in Mississippi. In 1977, the city of Mobile, Alabama, hired him as a resident artist. Since then, Smith has won 25 first place or Best of Show awards for his work, exhibiting his artwork all across the United States, including the National Museum of American Art at the Smithsonian Institution in Washington, DC, and the American Craft Museum in New York City. His pottery was also included in the traveling exhibit "Uncommon Beauty in Common Objects: The Legacy of African American Craft Art."

One of Charles Smith's unique pottery pieces.

Selling Pottery via YouTube

Artists always face the challenge of finding customers for their work. In Smith's case, he turned to the newest of today's new media: YouTube videos.

Smith and his son Ashanti made the decision to go with YouTube in late 2006. As Smith puts it:

I saw what was out there and noticed there was a void of African-American artists, and more specifically African-American potters, in the market. When I saw some of the other art-related videos [on YouTube], I felt it would be a good idea to put some of my own work out to the masses.

Smith's first video was a photo montage/slideshow that he and his son put together as a test to see what kind of response they would get. That video wasn't overly successful, so they took it down and replaced it with a demonstration video—a video that showed viewers how pottery is made.

The demonstration format was the key to success. The initial demonstration video gained a cadre of viewers who were interested not only in general pottery techniques, but also in the skills and the art of Charles Smith; it led to nine other videos that built on the first video's success.

Learning how to make pottery from artist Charles Smith.

The videos have directed many visitors back to Smith's freestanding website and have, in turn, provided extra opportunities for direct communication with new customers. Viewers of Smith's videos tend to be students and teachers of pottery, as well as art and pottery collectors. He relies on word of mouth to attract new viewers, and he uses the videos as part of other print and electronic promotions.

Making Educational Videos

Charles and Ashanti try to be as cost-efficient as possible when producing their videos. They've built their own video production studio and use it to produce all their YouTube videos in-house; they also produce videos for other clients. If they went outside for production, they'd probably spend a few thousand dollars for each video.

Each video allows Charles the freedom to express himself by throwing, building, and designing the pot as he is inspired to do so. They add a little wow factor by destroying each piece at the end of the video; this has been a trademark of Charles' demonstrations for years.

The result is more than the entertaining videos typically seen on YouTube; Smith's videos are more of a learning tool for aspiring artists and art lovers. Each video gives fans, clients, and customers of Charles Smith an opportunity to see the inside of what really goes into the formation of building a quality pot.

The key is to use the informative videos to draw viewers to the Charles Smith Pottery website, where Smith's artwork is available for sale. As Ashanti notes, "By mixing the YouTube videos with the promotion of the website, it increases the marketability and exposure of the pottery."

Advice for Other Businesses

Of course, Charles and Ashanti continue to develop their style from video to video. Ashanti offers this advice to other artists working with YouTube:

When you are dealing with the public, and you have people returning to you to see what you're going to do next, the demand grows for you to always be bigger and better than you were the last time. So as we continue to produce these videos, we must increase the quality, content, and approach. They now expect to be 'wowed' so we must try for another 'shocker.' Also, as the popularity of YouTube grows and advances, you have to know how to grow and advance with it. You always have to stay a step ahead.

As Charles and Ashanti note, you have to find your own style and then do whatever it takes to make your videos happen. If you stay true to yourself and your business and offer something educational and entertaining, you'll attract viewers—and customers.

Managing Your YouTube Videos

9

Uploading Your Videos to YouTube

You determined how YouTube fits into your online marketing mix. You decided what type of YouTube video to produce. You even made the video, edited it, and converted it to the proper video. Now it's time to upload your video to the YouTube site and put your message in front of millions of YouTube viewers.

Uploading Videos from Your Computer

Let's start at the top. Assuming that you shot your video with a camcorder, you transferred the video from your camcorder to your computer's hard disk, where you performed any necessary editing. The final video file you create is what you upload to YouTube.

Starting the Upload Process

To upload a video file, it must be in a YouTube-approved format, be less than 10 minutes long, and be smaller than 100MB. If your video meets these requirements, you're ready to upload.

note

Learn more about YouTube-approved video formats in Chapter 4, "Understanding Audio/Video Technology."

To upload a video, start by clicking the Upload button near the top-right corner of any YouTube page, as shown in Figure 9.1. This displays the Video Upload page; you now have a little paperwork to do.

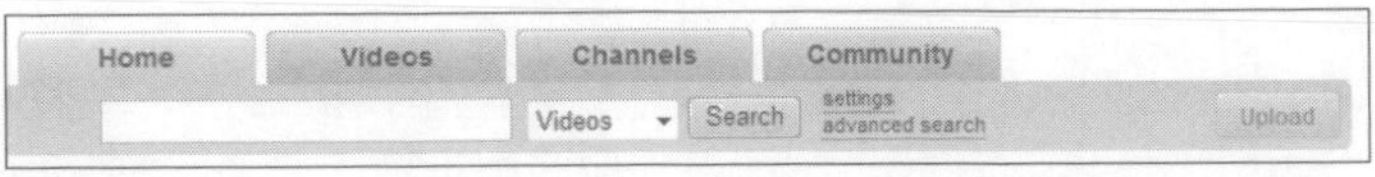

FIGURE 9.1

Click the Upload button to start uploading your video.

Entering Information About Your Video

When the Video Upload page appears, as shown in Figure 9.2, you must enter several bits of information about your video. After you enter the information requested on the Video Upload page, scroll to the bottom of the page and click the Upload a Video button.

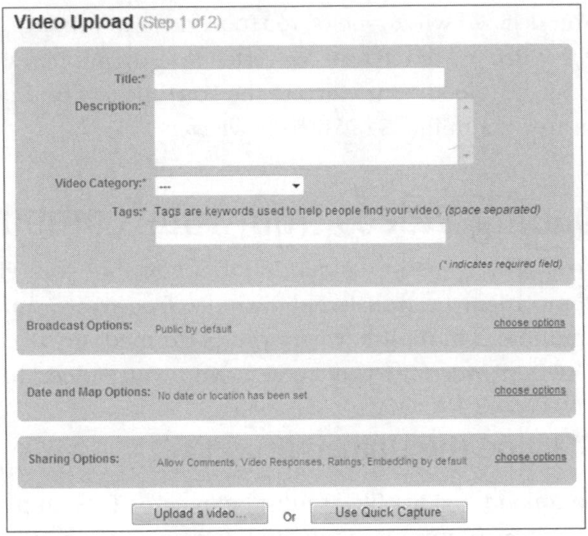

FIGURE 9.2

Entering information before you upload your video.

note

If you're capturing a video live from a webcam, click the Use Quick Capture button instead. Learn more in Chapter 5, "Shooting Webcam Videos."

Let's look at each type of information requested by YouTube.

Title

Start by entering a title for your video. The title should be descriptive without being overly long, as catchy as a traditional advertising headline. In fact, that's the best way to think of the title—like an ad headline.

Description

You now enter a description for the video. This can and should be longer and more complete than the shorter title. The description is also where you include the information that drives viewers to ask for more information or purchase what you're selling. That means including all or some of the following:

- Website address (URL)
- Toll-free telephone number
- Email address
- Mailing address (postal)

Although subtlety is important within the video itself, don't be quite so subtle when soliciting customers. Include all the information necessary for viewers to contact you about your product or service; don't be shy about asking for further contact.

Category

Next, select a category for your video from the pull-down list. From the following list, pick the category that best fits your video:

- Autos & Vehicles
- Comedy
- Education
- Entertainment
- Film & Animation
- Howto & Style
- Music
- News & Politics
- Nonprofits & Activism
- People & Blogs
- Pets & Animals

- Science & Technology
- Sports
- Travel & Events

Tags

Following the category selection, enter one or more tags for the video, separating each tag by a space. A *tag* is a keyword that viewers enter when searching the YouTube site. The tags you enter should be keywords that viewers might enter if they're looking for products or services like yours.

You can use as many tags as necessary to capture all possible search words. Your tags should include your company name, the topic of the video, and any other descriptive words or phrases.

Broadcast Options

The next three parameters are typically set in advance, although you can change any of the defaults by clicking the appropriate Change Options link. The first of these parameters are the broadcast options and determine whether the video is public (viewable by any YouTube user) or private (viewable by selected users only). The default option is public.

tip

Most videos for businesses should be set for public unless you have a private presentation or real estate walk-through you want to share with only selected clients.

Date and Map Options

These options, when enabled, display the date of the video's recording and the location of your business. This latter option lets users map your video—that is, display where your business is, geographically.

Sharing Options

These options enable you to allow or disallow text comments, video responses, viewer ratings, and embedding.

note

Learn more about sharing options in the "Dealing with Viewers and Viewer Comments" section of Chapter 10, "Creating a YouTube Presence."

Selecting the Video to Upload

Page two of the video upload process, shown in Figure 9.3, is where you specify the file to upload.

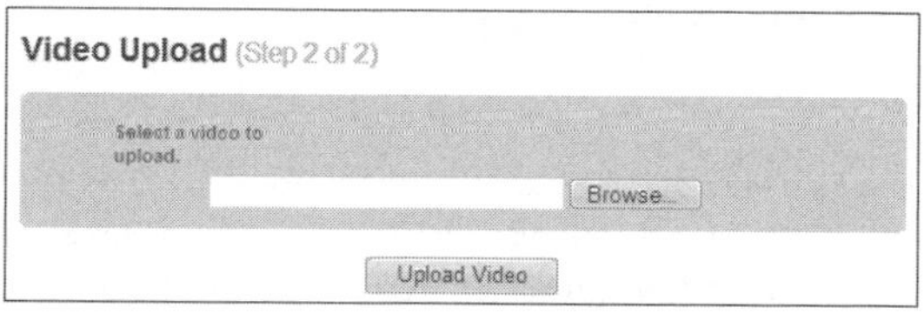

Video Upload (Step 2 of 2)

Select a video to upload.

[   ] [Browse...]

[Upload Video]

FIGURE 9.3

Page two of the video upload process.

Click the Browse button to open the Choose File dialog box, shown in Figure 9.4. Navigate to and select the file you want and then click Open. This loads the filename into the Select a Video to Upload box on the Video Upload page.

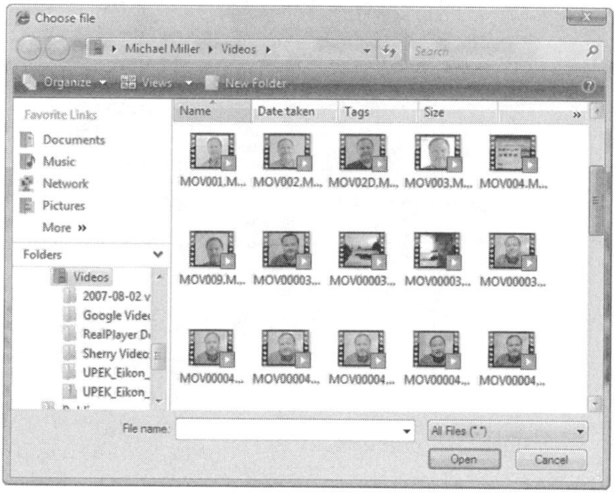

FIGURE 9.4

Selecting a video to upload.

Uploading the Video

When all of that is done, the final step is to click the Upload Video button. YouTube finds the video on your hard disk and starts uploading it; the Video Upload page shows the file's progress.

After you click the button, you need to be patient; it can take several minutes to upload a large video, especially over a slow Internet connection. There is additional processing time involved after the upload is complete, while YouTube converts the uploaded video to its own format and adds it to the YouTube database.

---

note

Videos you upload are not immediately available for viewing on YouTube. They must first be processed and approved by the site, which can take anywhere from a few minutes to a few hours.

When the video upload finishes, YouTube displays the Upload Complete page, shown in Figure 9.5. To view your video, click the My Videos link on any YouTube page and then click the thumbnail for your new video.

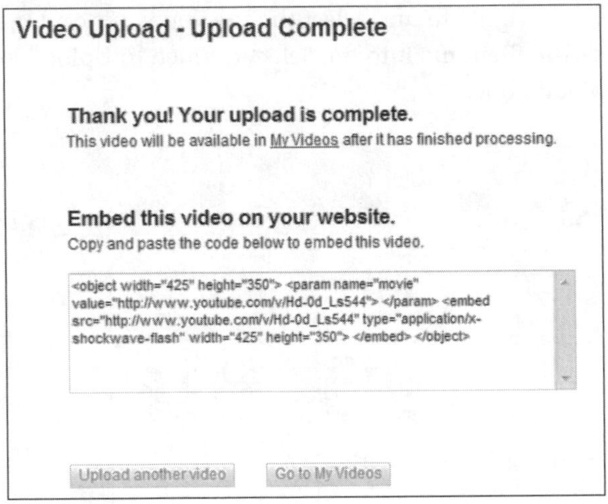

Video Upload - Upload Complete

Thank you! Your upload is complete.
This video will be available in My Videos after it has finished processing.

Embed this video on your website.
Copy and paste the code below to embed this video.

```
<object width="425" height="350"> <param name="movie"
value="http://www.youtube.com/v/Hd-0d_Ls544"> </param> <embed
src="http://www.youtube.com/v/Hd-0d_Ls544" type="application/x-
shockwave-flash" width="425" height="350"> </embed> </object>
```

Upload another video   Go to My Videos

FIGURE 9.5

Congratulations—your upload is complete!

---

tip

The Upload Complete page includes the HTML code necessary to embed the video on your own web page or blog. Just copy and paste the code into your page's raw HTML to make the addition.

Editing Video Information

After you uploaded your video to YouTube, you can edit all information about your video. All you have to do is click the My Videos link on the YouTube home page. This displays a list of all the videos you've uploaded, as shown in Figure 9.6. From here, click the Edit Video Info button beside the video you want to edit.

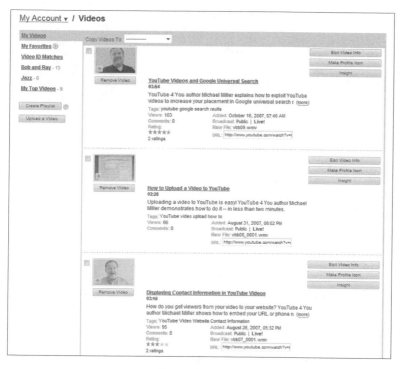

FIGURE 9.6

Click the Edit Video Info button to edit information for a specific video.

The fun begins when the Edit My Video page appears. As you can see in Figure 9.7, this page looks almost identical to the original Video Upload information page. You can edit all information fields listed here, including the video's title, description, category tags, and so on. Click the Update Video Info button when you finish making changes.

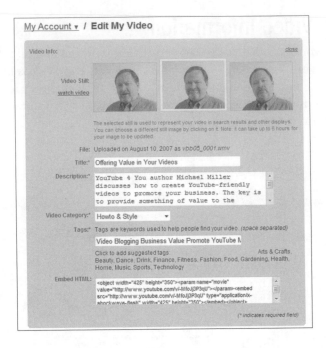

FIGURE 9.7
Editing information about your video.

---

tip

What can you do if you don't like the thumbnail image that YouTube chooses for your video? Just go to the Edit My Video and choose one of the three preselected thumbnail images at the top of the page.

Removing a Video from YouTube

When a video has run its course, you can remove it from the YouTube site; otherwise, it stays online forever (or until YouTube goes out of business, whichever comes first).

To remove a video from YouTube, click the My Videos link on the YouTube home page to display the list of all your videos; click the Remove Video button below the video you want to delete. It's that simple.

---

caution

Think twice before you click the Remove Video button. YouTube permanently deletes all the videos you remove. You have to re-upload the video if you click the Remove Video button by mistake.

The Big Picture

Assuming that you prepared your video properly, uploading a video file to YouTube is a simple task. The hardest part is filling in all the blanks. It's important to write a catchy title and detailed description, as well as to choose tags and keywords that viewers might use to search for your video.

When you upload your video to YouTube, approach it in the same way you would create a print advertisement. You have to create a compelling headline (title) and a "why to buy" and "how to buy" description. Then you have to select the best place to market your ad/video (category) and the best keywords to get your video notice (tags). This isn't a job to do at the last minute without any preparation; you want your best marketing people working on the textual part of your YouTube videos. ■

10

Creating a YouTube Presence

YouTube is more than just a source of videos; it's a community. The community aspects of the site help you build viewership and a customer base, and establish your own unique business presence. That's right, being successful on YouTube isn't just about creating a great video; you also have to take advantage of the social nature of the YouTube site to build a community of friends and subscribers.

Working with Channels

The most common way to participate in the YouTube community is by using YouTube's channels. On YouTube, *channel* is just a fancy name for a user's profile. As soon as you post your first video, you create your own YouTube channel. At that point, other users can access your channel to see all the videos you've uploaded; users can also subscribe to your channel to receive notification when you upload new videos to the YouTube site.

Viewing a Channel Profile

YouTube viewers access your channel page to learn more about you and to connect with your business. A viewer accesses your channel by clicking your business's name wherever it appears on the YouTube site. Although each profile page is unique, all pages contain the same major elements, as shown in Figure 10.1:

- Information about the user, including a link to subscribe to this channel

- Videos uploaded by this user
- Links to connect to the user, via email, comments, and so on—including a link to the user's non-YouTube website
- Links to the user's favorite videos, playlists, groups, friends, and the like
- Subscribers to the user's channel
- Comments on this user's channel
- The user's favorite videos
- Channels the user is watching

FIGURE 10.1

A typical YouTube channel page.

If a viewer likes what he sees on your channel page, he can *subscribe* to that channel. When a viewer subscribes to you channel, he is automatically notified (via email) when you upload new videos.

Personalizing Your YouTube Channel

Because a YouTube channel page is actually a profile page, you want to customize your page to reflect your business's image and brand. It's easy to do.

As for creating your channel page, there's nothing to do; YouTube creates a profile page for you when you subscribe to the site. The default channel page is a little bland, however, which is why you want to customize it.

You personalize your channel page from your My Account page. Just click the Account link at the top of any YouTube page, and when the My Account page appears, scroll to the My Channel section, shown in Figure 10.2.

FIGURE 10.2

Getting ready to personalize your channel profile page.

From here you can edit the following channel elements:

- **Channel Info**—As shown in Figure 10.3, you can enter a new title and description for your channel page. You can also configure how to handle comments and bulletins, as well as the channel type.
- **Channel Design**—As shown in Figure 10.4, this is where you change the overall look and feel of your channel page. You can select a new color scheme for your page; opt to show or hide various page elements; and choose custom colors for selected page elements, as well as a background image for your page.

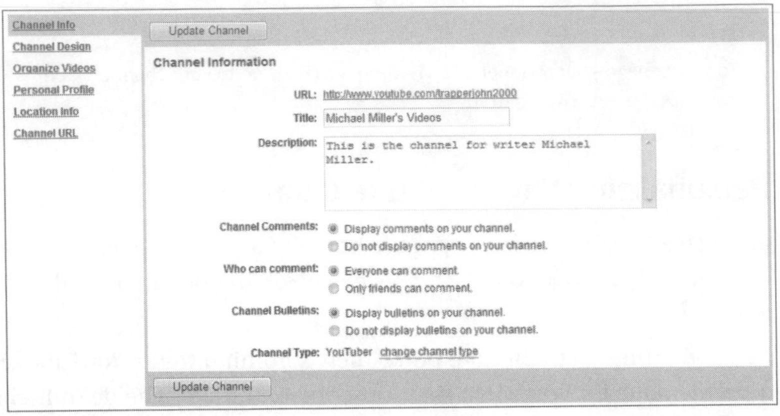

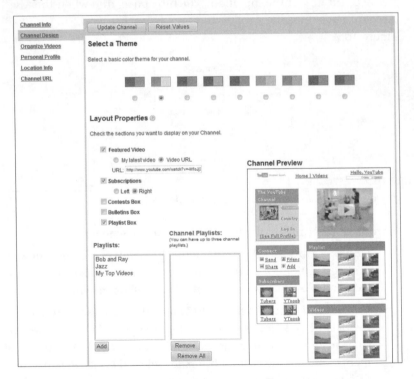

FIGURE 10.3

Customizing your channel info.

FIGURE 10.4

Personalizing the design of your channel page.

- **Organize Videos**—As shown in Figure 10.5, this page lets you organize the order of the first nine videos shown on your channel page.

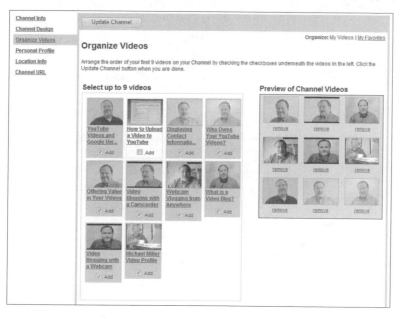

FIGURE 10.5

Customizing the order of the videos shown on your channel page.

- **Personal Profile**—As shown in Figure 10.6, this page lets you enter personal or business information to be displayed on your channel page, such as your business name, description, link to your outside website, and so on. You can also choose a picture or video still to display at the top of your channel page.
- **Location Info**—As shown in Figure 10.7, this is where you enter your hometown, current city, ZIP code, and country.

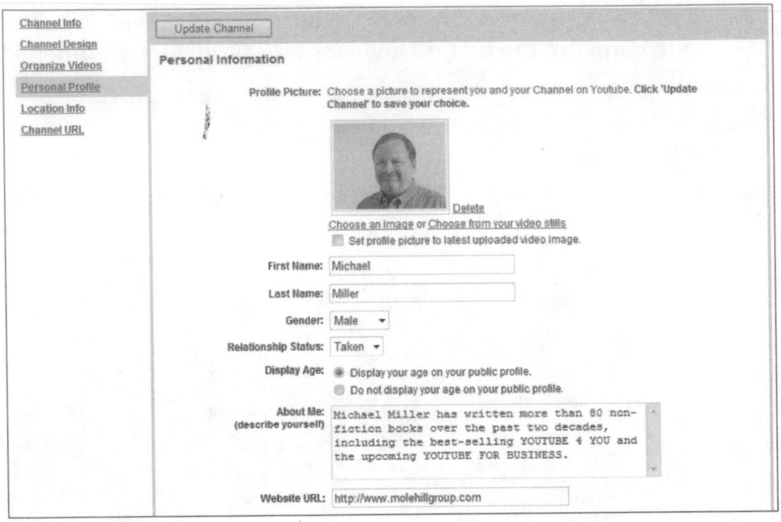

FIGURE 10.6

Adding relevant information to your channel page.

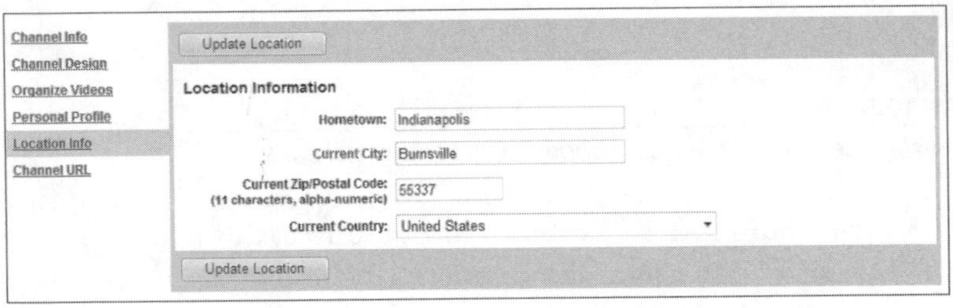

FIGURE 10.7

Adding your location to your channel page.

- **Channel URL**—As shown in Figure 10.8, this page displays the URL for your channel page.

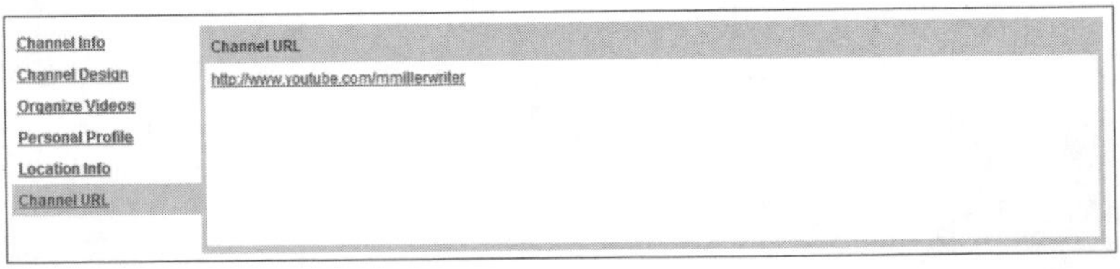

FIGURE 10.8

Viewing your channel URL.

As you make changes to any page element, make sure you click the Update Channel button, or you'll lose the changes you made.

Managing Your Channel's Video Log

One cool feature that you can add to your channel page is a video log or *vlog*. A vlog is an easy way for you to create a personal video journal accessible to anyone visiting your channel.

To create a vlog, go to the YouTube home page and click the My Playlists link in the My box. When the Playlists page appears, you can choose to select an existing playlist as your vlog or create a new playlist to hold new vlog entries. To use an existing playlist, select the playlist and then click the Set as Video Log button. To create a new vlog playlist, click the Create Playlist button to create the new playlist and make sure you check the Use This Playlist as Video Log in My Channel option.

Your vlog now appears on your channel profile page. The individual videos in the vlog playlist stack on top of each other; visitors can click a video to view it.

YouTube Channel Marketing

YouTube thrives on social networking—and your channel and videos get more viewers if you fully participate in the YouTube community. You can't just post some videos and expect to get viewers automatically; you have to make your presence known to inform viewers of the videos you posted.

In reality, this means being an active viewer as well as a poster. You become a member of the community when you view and subscribe to a lot of other channels; you become even more noticed when you leave comments with those videos and users that best serve your needs.

How does this work in reality? It takes time and effort. You want to search the YouTube site for videos like yours, or users who have something in common with your business. After you find a sympathetic user, view his videos and leave some comments. You might want to mention that you have similar videos in your channel and encourage friends of this user to head over to your channel to see more. At the very least, you want to spark interest in your videos from the person whose videos you're viewing. If you view his videos, he'll view yours, and hopefully tell other viewers about what he saw.

What goes around comes around; the more comments you leave, the more people see your name and channel and the more views your videos receive. To get people interested in your channel, you have to show interest in theirs.

Working with Groups

Another form of community on YouTube is the YouTube groups feature. A *group* is a social forum where users interested in a given topic can share videos and conduct online discussions.

Groups are useful in a marketing context because they formalize a virtual community. If you find a group that focuses on the type of product or service you offer, that group is a natural conduit for viewers and future customers. In fact, you can recruit some loyal and vocal customers from YouTube's groups; these folks are among the most rabid fans you're likely to encounter!

Joining an Existing Group

To find YouTube groups, click the Community tab on the home page and then click the Groups link located toward the top of the page. This displays a list of featured groups and contests.

When you access a group page, like the one shown in Figure 10.9, you see links to group videos, members, and discussions. The page displays recent videos and the most recent group discussions.

To join a group, simply click the Join This Group link. After you join a group, you can participate in group discussions, add videos to the group, and so forth.

One of the most addictive features of a YouTube group is its discussion pages. This is where group members meet to discuss the topic at hand; it's a great way to get face-to-face contact with potential customers. To join a group discussion, just click the Discussions link on the group page; this displays a discussion page, such as the one shown in Figure 10.10. You can then read comments within that discussion or add your own comment from the Add New Comment section at the bottom of the page.

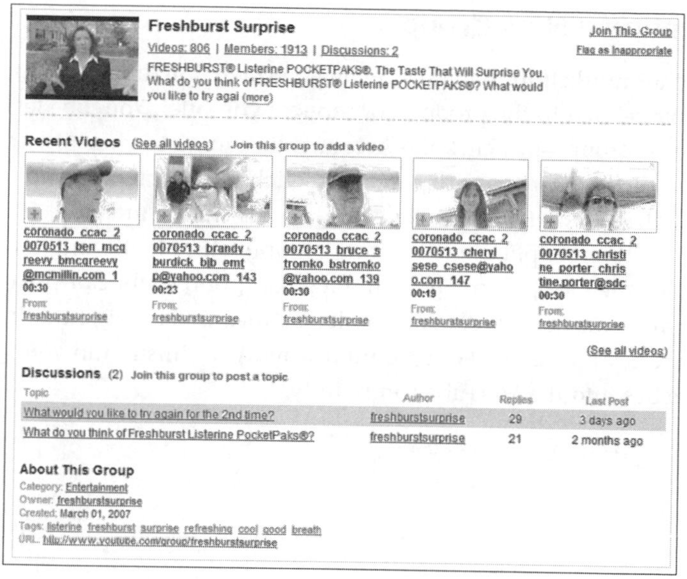

FIGURE 10.9

A YouTube group page for Listerine's FreshBurst Surprise brand.

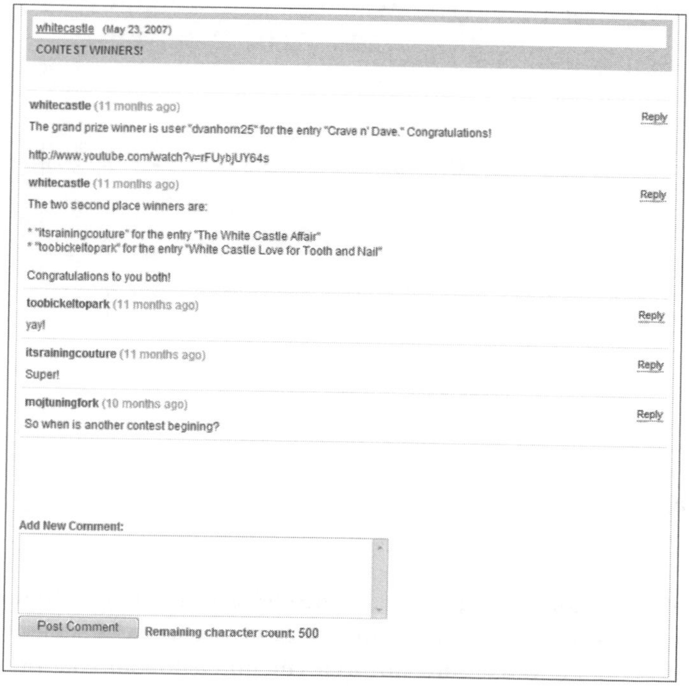

FIGURE 10.10

Joining in the discussion at the White Castle Craver Video Contest group.

Creating a New Group

Another marketing ploy is to create your own YouTube group, focused on a topic related to the products or services you offer. YouTube lets anyone create a group—just click the Accounts link to go to your My Accounts page, click the Groups link, and then click the Create a Group button. When the Create a Group page appears, as shown in Figure 10.11, enter a name and description for the group, along with identifying tags, a custom URL for the group, a category, the type of group (public or private), and how you want to handle video uploads, forum postings, and the group icon. Click the Create Group button when you finish, and your group launches into the YouTube community.

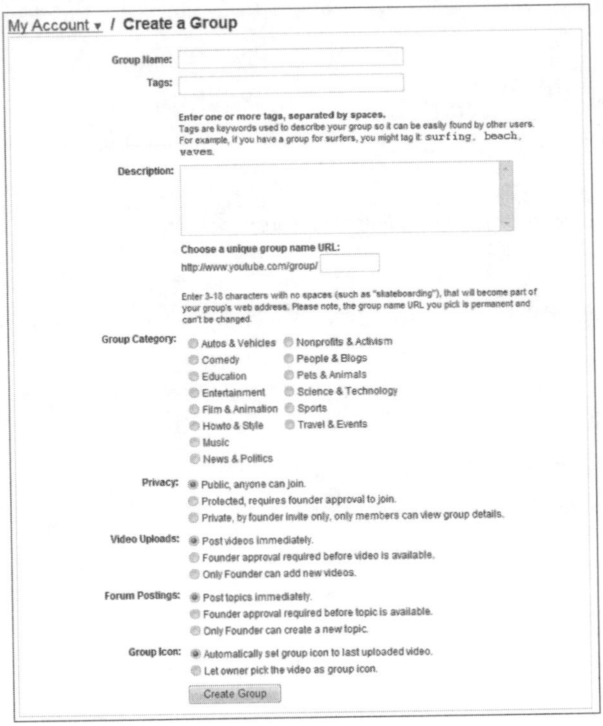

FIGURE 10.11

Creating a new YouTube group.

After you create your group, you need to recruit members to it—ideally, other users that share the group interest. Click the Invite Members link at the top right of the group page to invite others to join your group. This displays the page shown in Figure 10.12; you can invite members of your Friends list or invite other members by entering their member names in the New Friends list. Click the Send button to send your invitations.

tip

You can find potential group members via searching or from their membership in other similar groups.

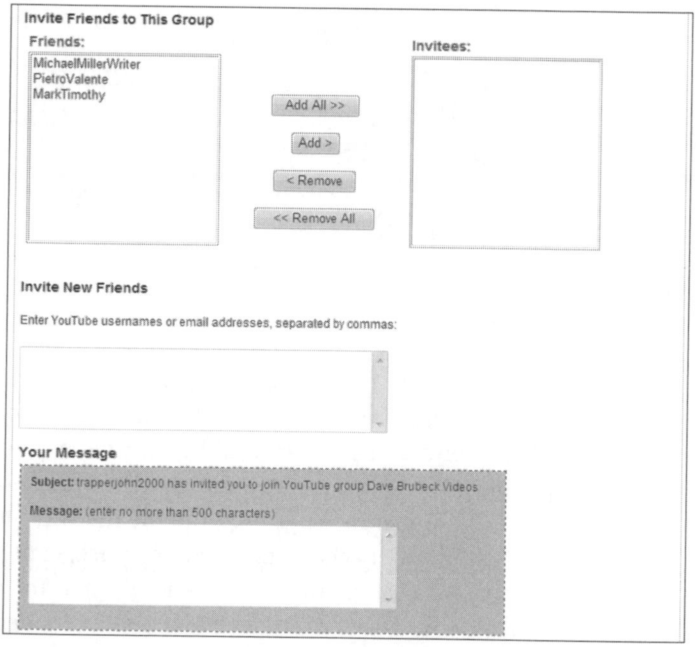

FIGURE 10.12

Inviting other YouTubers to join your group.

Click the Add Videos link at the top right of the group page to add videos to your group. This displays a page with links to your current favorite videos and playlists, as shown in Figure 10.13. Check any video you want to add; then click the Add to Group button. Alternatively, you can click the Upload a Video button to upload a new video and add it to your group.

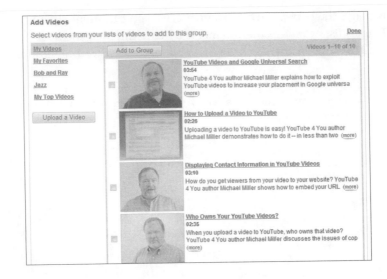

FIGURE 10.13

Adding videos to your new group.

There are many ways to use a YouTube group in your marketing mix. One of the most popular approaches is to create some sort of contest revolving around your brand or product, and then create a group to support that contest. This lets you keep your main channel free and clear for your ongoing brand or product message; you handle the short-term contest purely through the group mechanism. And, of course, contests are great ways to involve your customer base—especially when they involve the creation of videos about your brand or product, all uploaded to YouTube!

tip

If you advertise on the YouTube site (outside of the videos you upload), you can feature your contest in YouTube's official Contests section. To learn more about advertising on YouTube, email ads@youtube.com.

Working with Friends and Contacts

You don't have to create a group to mingle with potential customers on YouTube. That's because YouTube lets you create lists of users with whom you can share your videos. YouTube's Friends list is kind of like a buddy list in AOL Instant Messenger; one click on a YouTube list lets you share your videos with everyone on your list.

You can think of YouTube's Friends list as a kind of high-tech customer mailing list. When you have something portentous to announce to your customers (such as a new video or a product introduction), you can send out a message to your list. Unlike traditional customer mailings, however, sending electronic messages to your YouTube friends list is completely free.

Adding a Friend to Your List

Adding an existing YouTube member to your friends list is relatively easy. Just go to that member's channel or profile page, scroll to the Connect With box, shown in Figure 10.14, and click the Add as Friend link. YouTube now sends an invitation to this person to be your friend; if he accepts, YouTube adds him to your Friends list.

FIGURE 10.14

Adding an existing YouTube member to your Friends list.

You can also add friends who aren't yet YouTube members. Just click the Account link at the top of any YouTube page to display the My Account page; then scroll down to the Contacts & Subscribers section, shown in Figure 10.15, and click the Invite Friends button.

FIGURE 10.15

Managing friends and contacts from your My Account page.

When the Invite Your Friends page appears, as shown in Figure 10.16, enter the email addresses of those folks you want to invite (separate each address with a comma), and then click the Send Invite button. The friends you entered receive official email invitations; they can click the link in the email message to join YouTube and add themselves to your Friends list.

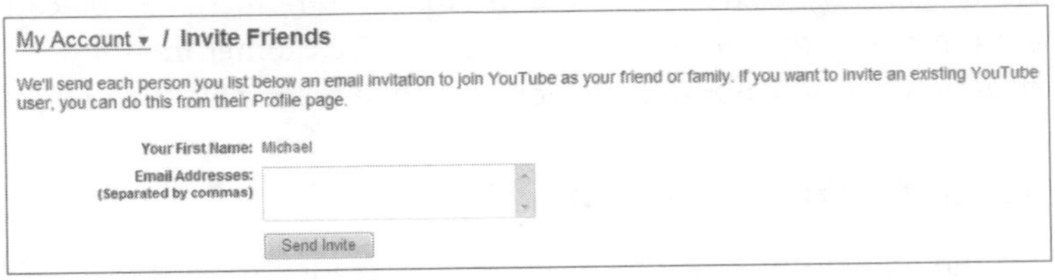

FIGURE 10.16

Inviting a non-YouTuber to join your Friends list.

Sending Messages to Your Friends

When you want to send a message to someone in your Friends list, go to your My Account page, scroll down to the Contacts & Subscribers section, and click the My Contacts link. As you can see in Figure 10.17, this lists all your contacts. Click the Send Message link next to a friend's name; this displays the Compose Message page shown in Figure 10.18. Enter a subject for your message and the text of the message itself. If you want to attach a YouTube video to this message, pull down the Attach a Video list and choose a video from your favorites. Click the Send Message button to send the message on its way.

FIGURE 10.17

Viewing all your YouTube contacts.

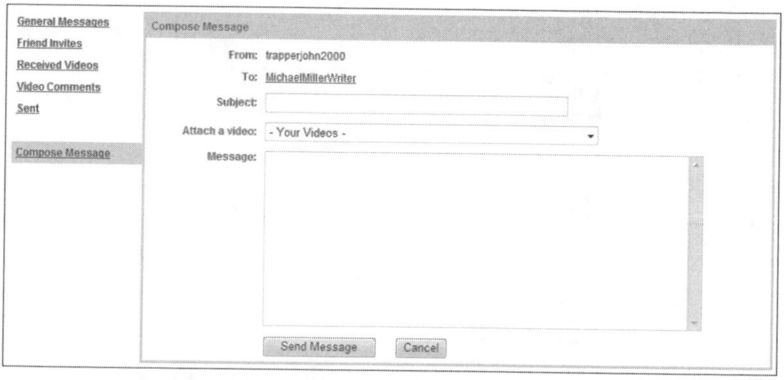

FIGURE 10.18

Sending a message to a friend.

tip

You're not limited to sending messages to only existing friends and contacts. To send a message to any YouTube user, go to your inbox and click the Compose New Message button; from there you can enter any member's username for the message you compose.

Reading Messages from Other Users

YouTube also lets you receive messages from your viewers and customers; these messages end up in your YouTube inbox. You access your inbox by going to YouTube's home page and clicking the My Inbox link in the My box. As you can see in Figure 10.19, your inbox lists, under the General Messages link, all email messages you've received. You can view other types of messages by clicking the Friend Invites, Received Videos, Video Comments, Video Responses, and Sent links.

To read a message, just click it in your inbox; the message displays onscreen. You can delete the message, mark it as spam, or send a reply to the message by using the Your Reply box and the Send Message button.

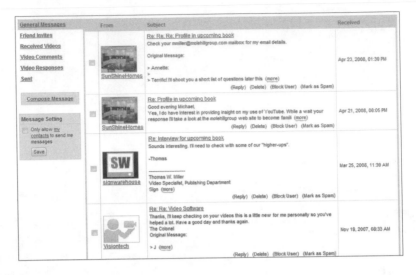

FIGURE 10.19

Waiting messages in your YouTube inbox.

Dealing with Viewers and Viewer Comments

One of the fun things about marketing via YouTube is that you get to immediately see the comments and responses from people who view your videos. Although this can be fun, it isn't always pleasant, which is why YouTube lets you manage these comments.

Enabling Comments, Video Responses, Ratings, Embedding, and Syndication

Viewers can leave both text comments and video responses to your videos—if you let them. At your discretion, you can allow, disallow, or allow with prior approval either comments or video responses for any individual video you upload. (This means you can allow comments for one video and disallow comments for another.)

To control comments and video responses, click the My Videos link on the YouTube home page to display the list of all your videos. Then click the Edit Video Info button below the video you want to control. When the Edit My Video page appears, scroll down to the Sharing Options section, and then click the Choose Options link; this expands the section, as shown in Figure 10.20. You can configure six options, as discussed next.

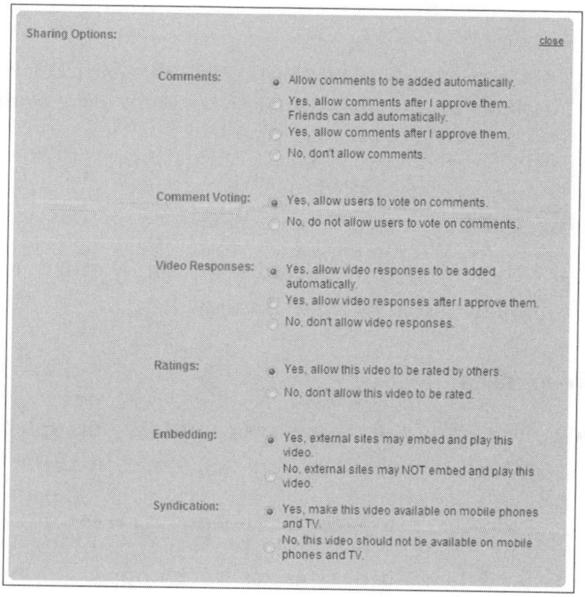

FIGURE 10.20

Enabling or disabling comments and video responses.

Comments

By default, anyone viewing your video can leave text comments about the video. The options you have for accepting comments include the following:

- **Allow Comments to Be Added Automatically**—Viewers can submit text comments, which appear immediately on your video page.

- **Yes, Allow Comments After I Approve Them. Friends Can Add Automatically**—Viewers can submit text comments, but you have to approve each comment before it appears on your video page—unless the viewer is part of your preapproved Friends list.

- **Yes, Allow Comments After I Approve Them**—All comments, even those from friends, have to be preapproved.

- **No, Don't Allow Comments**—The Comments section does not appear on your video page.

> **tip**
>
> Allowing video comments might be desirable if you want your customers to copy, edit, remix, enhance, or even make fun of your videos—all of which are valid ways to encourage customer interaction.

Comment Voting

This feature lets viewers vote on comments left by other viewers. Select Yes to allow comment voting or No to disallow it.

Video Responses

When you enable this option, viewers can make and upload their own videos in response to your video. You can choose from the following options:

- **Yes, Allow Video Responses to Be Added Automatically**—Viewers can upload their video responses, which appear immediately on your video page.
- **Yes, Allow Video Responses After I Approve Them**—Any video responses have to be approved by you before they appear on your video page.
- **No, Don't Allow Video Responses**—The video response option does not appear on your video page.

Ratings

In lieu of (or in addition to) detailed text comments, you can also allow your video to be rated by viewers. Viewers can rate videos on a scale of one to five stars, with five stars being the best and one star being the worst.

> **tip**
>
> To view the rating for your video, go to that video's page and scroll to the options box below the video player; the current star rating displays there.

You have the option of not allowing viewers to rate your video. This might be desirable if you don't want your business's videos perceived in a negative fashion. On the other hand, if you have a popular video, you probably want to enable ratings—highly rated videos rank higher in YouTube search results than do poorly rated ones.

Your option in regard to ratings is simple: Check Yes to allow ratings or No to disallow them.

Embedding

YouTube makes it easy for any user to embed your video in his or her own website or blog. If you want wider exposure for your video, check Yes to display the embeddable HTML code. If, on the other hand, your lawyers tell you that you need to keep complete control over where and how users view your video, click No to hide the embeddable code.

---

tip

I can think of no good reason not to allow embedding, unless you have a legal staff paranoid about copyright and fair usage. If you want to create a truly viral video, you have to allow fans to embed the video across the Web.

Syndication

You can achieve even wider viewership by making your video accessible to viewers on mobile phones and TV. YouTube dubs this added exposure *syndication*, and you can turn it on or off for any specific video.

Approving Comments and Video Responses

If you choose the "with approval" option for comments or video responses, you have to manually approve any comments or responses viewers post to this video. When a viewer posts a comment or response, YouTube sends you an email like the one in Figure 10.21. Thus notified, go to the YouTube site and click the email link at the top of any YouTube page, and then click the Text Comments link or the Video Responses link.

As you can see in Figure 10.22, clicking the respective link displays a list of all pending comments/responses in your inbox.

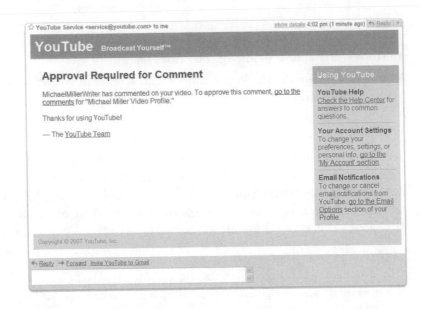

FIGURE 10.21
YouTube sends an email notification when you receive a comment or response to your video.

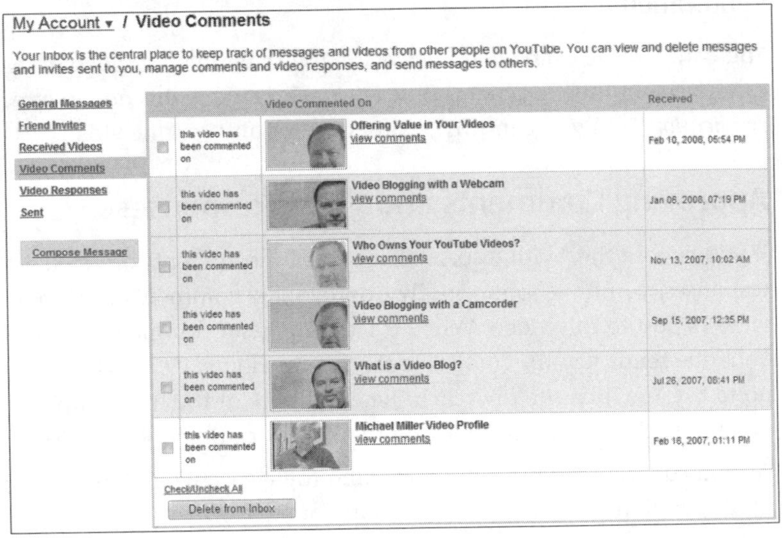

FIGURE 10.22
Pending comments and responses in your YouTube inbox.

Click the message link to display the comment, as shown in Figure 10.23.

FIGURE 10.23

Responding to a viewer comment.

From here you can choose from the following options:

- **Reply**—Click to post a reply to a viewer comment.
- **Remove**—Click to disallow a pending comment or remove a previously approved comment.
- **Block User**—Click to block a user from posting future comments.
- **Approve**—Click to approve and post this specific comment to your video page. Available only if you choose the Allow Comments After I Approve Them option in your video setup.
- **Spam**—Click to report this comment to YouTube as spam.

To approve a comment or response to your video, click the Approve link. To not approve a comment, click the Remove link.

Dealing with Negative Comments

When you let viewers comment on your videos, you're opening a Pandora's Box. Yes, you'll receive some positive comments from satisfied viewers, but you'll also receive some negative comments—some of which might be downright nasty.

Some companies want to see only positive comments, which is valid. Other companies don't mind the negatives because they feel it presents a forthright, warts-and-all image to the market. There's no right or wrong here. Just know that if you enable comments, you *will* receive some negative ones. How you respond to those negative comments depends on how your company deals with criticism.

Removing Viewer Comments and Responses

One way to deal with negative comments is simply to remove them. As you previously learned, you can remove viewer comments and responses from the Text Comments and Video Responses sections of your YouTube inbox. You can also remove comments from the video page, which might be an easier thing to do if you have a ton of comments on a particular video.

To remove a comment in this fashion, go to the video page, find the comment or video response you want to remove, and then click the Remove link beneath that comment or response, as shown in Figure 10.24. Easy!

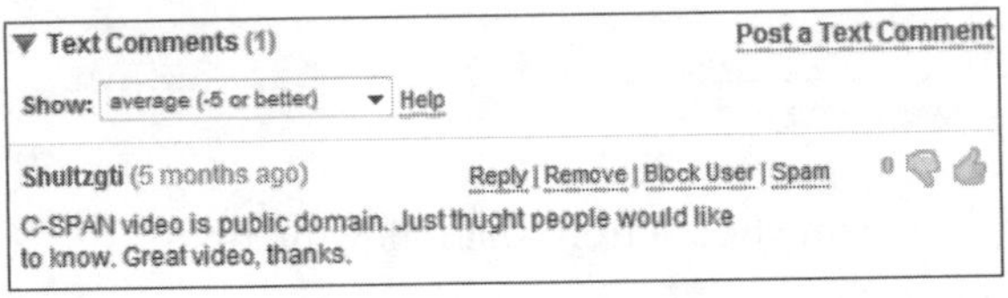

FIGURE 10.24
Removing an unwanted comment—click the Remove link.

Blocking Members from Leaving Comments

Every now and then you run into a virtual stalker, a disgruntled customer (or perhaps a competitor) who delights in leaving negative comments on all your videos. Although you can manually remove all of this user's comments, a better approach is to keep him from leaving those comments in the first place.

To this end, YouTube enables you to block individual members from leaving comments and responses (and from flooding your YouTube inbox with negative messages). To block a user, all you have to do is click that member's name to access his channel page, scroll to the Connect With box, and click the Block User link. This blocks the user from commenting on your videos and contacting you.

tip
You can also block a user directly from the video page. Just click the Block User link under that user's comments.

Unsubscribing Users from Your Channel

In addition to blocking user comments, you might also want to get rid of unwelcome subscribers to your video channel. You do this by clicking the Account link at the top of any YouTube page; when the My Account page appears, scroll down to the Contacts & Subscribers section and click the My Subscribers link. This displays a list of members subscribed to your videos, as shown in Figure 10.25. To remove a subscriber, simply click the Unsubscribe link under the subscriber's name.

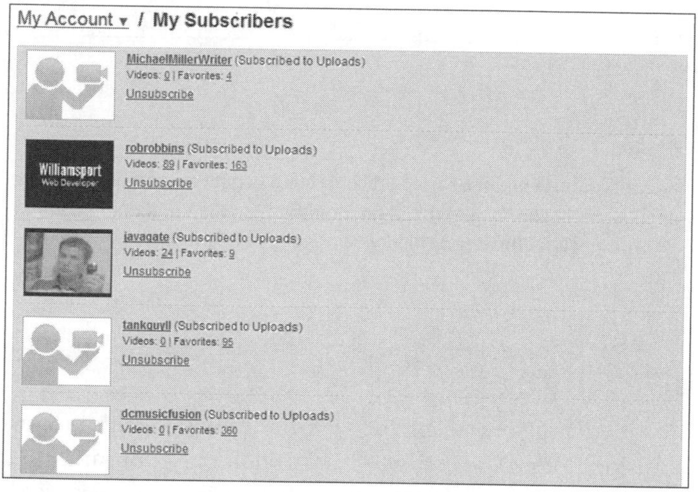

FIGURE 10.25

Removing a subscriber to your video channel.

Responding to Negative Comments

Another way to deal with negative comments is to deal with them head on by responding directly. YouTube lets you add your own responses to any comments left about your videos; this can be a good forum for exchanging views and opinions with your customer base.

To respond to a message, go to the video page and scroll down to the Commentary section under the video window; you should see a list of all viewer comments. Find the comment to which you want to reply and then click the Reply link. This displays a reply box, as shown in Figure 10.26. Enter your reply into this box, and then click the Post Comment button. Your reply displays directly beneath the comment in question.

FIGURE 10.26

Replying to a viewer's comments.

caution

Your best recourse might be *not* to respond to a negative comment. When you enter your reply, you run the risk of fanning the fires of a burgeoning flame war, from which neither the disgruntled viewer nor you might come off looking good.

The Big Picture

Taking advantage of the YouTube community is essential to promoting your business or online content. It's through these community ties that you drive viewers to your videos and then on to your own website.

Of course, participating in the YouTube community requires a real commitment; it's not something you can do halfway or hire someone to do. (YouTubers can spot a "hired gun" from a mile away.) You have to take the time to learn the YouTube community and actively participate in it. That means viewing lots of videos, entering lots of thoughtful comments, and joining lots of groups. It can be a full-time job.

You also have to determine how you want to respond to the inevitable negative comments posted about your videos. You can choose to ignore the negative comments, reply to them, or just delete them. You can also choose to skip the issue entirely by not enabling the comments feature for your videos. If your company is particularly thin-skinned or you think your videos might generate particularly controversial responses, this might be the way to go. ■

11

Incorporating YouTube Videos on Your Own Website

YouTube is a great place to display your company's videos, but you can display the videos you create for YouTube on your own website or blog, too. And the great thing is, you don't have to host them—YouTube does all the hosting and handles all the traffic for you!

With that in mind, let's look at the various ways to incorporate your YouTube videos into your company's website or blog. It's easy!

Adding YouTube Video Links to a Web Page

Not all companies want to include videos on their official websites. Instead, you might want to reference your YouTube videos without displaying them.

The easiest way to do this is via a link to a specific video on the YouTube site. Every YouTube video has its own unique web address or URL (*uniform resource locator*). You can copy and paste that URL into your company's web page or into email messages, blog postings, and the like.

Linking to an Individual Video

As just mentioned, every video on YouTube has its own unique web address. When you navigate to a video page, its URL is in the Address box in your web browser.

To insert the link into a web page, copy the URL from your browser's Address box and insert it into your page's underlying HTML code, surrounded by the appropriate link tag. The resulting code should look something like this, although on a single line:

```
Click <a href="http//:www.youtube.com/watch?v=12345">here</a>
 to view my YouTube video.
```

Naturally, replace the `href` link with the URL of the video you're linking to. When visitors click the link in the text, they go to that video's YouTube page.

> **tip**
>
> To insert a YouTube video link into an email message or blog post, simply copy the URL from the video page and paste it into the body of the message.

Linking to Your YouTube Channel—Or List of Videos

YouTube also lets you link to your YouTube channel page. Just use this URL within your link code:

```
http://www.youtube.com/user/username
```

Alternatively, you can link to a list of your uploaded videos using this URL:

```
http://www.youtube.com/videos/username
```

In both instances, replace *username* with your YouTube username.

> **tip**
>
> You can also link to any playlist you create. Just go to your My Playlists page, select the playlist, and copy the URL in the URL box. To embed all the videos in a playlist, copy the Embed link instead.

Embedding YouTube Videos in a Web Page

Linking to your YouTube videos is good, but embedding one or more of your videos on your own website is even better. That's right; YouTube lets you insert any of your videos into your own website, complete with video player window.

The best thing about embedding a YouTube video on your site is that you don't have to host the video on your site or handle the bandwidth when someone views the video. All you have to do is insert the proper code into your web page; the code references back to the YouTube site, which hosts the video. Visitors think they're viewing the video from your web page, but YouTube is actually serving the video to the visitor. You don't have to dedicate any storage space or bandwidth to the video.

Embedding a Basic Video

The process of embedding a video on your website is actually quite easy. That's because YouTube automatically creates the embed code for every public video on its site (as well as your own private videos), and lists this code on the video page itself. The code is in the information box at the top right of the video page, as shown in Figure 11.1. You'll need to copy this entire code (it's longer than the Embed box itself) and then paste it into the HTML code on your website.

FIGURE 11.1

The embed code for a YouTube video.

The embed code, when properly formatted, looks something like this:

```
<object width="425" height="350">
    <param name="movie"
    value="http://www.youtube.com/v/12345"></param>
    <param name="wmode" value="transparent"></param>
    <embed src="http://www.youtube.com/v/12345"
    type="application/x-shockwave-flash" wmode="transparent"
    width="425"
    height="350">
    </embed>
</object>
```

caution

Don't copy *this* code to your web page—it's just an example!

Insert the embed code into your web page's HTML where you want the video player window to display. What you get is a special click-to-play YouTube video player window, like the one shown in Figure 11.2, in line on your web page. The video itself remains stored on and served from YouTube's servers; only the code resides on your website. When a site visitor clicks the video, YouTube's servers deliver it to your viewer's web browser, just as if your own server sent it.

FIGURE 11.2
A click-to-play YouTube video window on your website.

tip

By default, a visitor has to click the embedded video to play it. To turn a click-to-play video into an autoplay video, insert the following code directly after both instances of the video's URL (no space between and before the end quotation mark): **&autoplay=1**.

Customizing the Embedded Video Player

When you use the standard embed code, YouTube embeds the default version of its video player on your web page. However, there are many ways to customize this player, which you might want to do to better blend the player into your web page.

To create a custom video player, click the Customize link above the Embed link on the YouTube video page. This expands the Information box with a bevy of options, as shown in Figure 11.3.

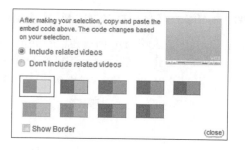

FIGURE 11.3

Customizing YouTube's embedded video player.

Here's what you can configure:

- **Include/Don't Include Related Videos**—By default, YouTube displays a list of related videos after your video finishes playing. If you don't want to show these videos, which will no doubt include videos from other users, check the Don't Include Related Videos option.

- **Themes**—Choose from nine different color schemes; pick the one that best matches the colors of your web page.

- **Show Border**—When you check this option, YouTube displays a border around the video player, as shown in Figure 11.4.

FIGURE 11.4

An embedded video player customized with a different color scheme and border.

When you select an option, the embed code automatically changes to reflect your choice. Just copy and embed this new code to create the custom video player on your website.

Embedding a Video List in Your Web Page

YouTube also lets you embed a scrolling list of your YouTube videos on your website, like the one shown in Figure 11.5. Your site's visitors can click any video in the list to view the video on YouTube.

FIGURE 11.5

A scrolling list of your YouTube videos for your web page.

To create this type of scrolling list, simply insert the following code into your web page HTML:

```
<iframe id="videos_list" name="videos_list"
src="http://www.youtube.com/videos_list?user=username"
scrolling="auto" width="265" height="300" frameborder="0"
marginheight="0" marginwidth="0">
</iframe>
```

Make sure you replace *username* with your own YouTube username.

tip

If you're a website developer, YouTube offers a set of tools, called the GoogleData Application Programming Interface (GData API), which lets you develop web-based applications using YouTube videos. Learn more at code.google.com/apis/youtube/.

The Big Picture

YouTube videos aren't just for YouTube viewers. You can offer your YouTube videos to visitors to your website either by including a link to your videos or by embedding specific videos on your web pages. YouTube makes it easy to do, just by including a short piece of HTML code. You can even customize the video player window to better match the look and feel of your company's web pages.

The nice thing about all this is that YouTube does all the hosting for you. If you run a small business and have only a limited amount of storage space and bandwidth for your website, you won't tap out your resources if your video becomes a hit. YouTube hosts the video and provides all the bandwidth necessary to view it—no matter how many viewers your video attracts. Viewers will think they're viewing the video on your website, but in reality YouTube is doing all the heavy lifting! ■

Profile: Annette Lawrence, ReMax ACR Elite Group, Inc.

I think that YouTube has particular potential for the real estate market. It just makes sense that a video tour of a property would be more appealing than a few static pictures. Wouldn't you prefer a video walkthrough of a house you might be interested in purchasing?

Some realtors recognize the potential and are getting ahead of the curve. One of these forward-thinking real estate agents is Annette Lawrence, who is using YouTube to promote those communities that she services and attract potential purchasers.

Company Profile

Company: Annette Lawrence, Realtor

Product: Real estate

YouTube channel: www.youtube.com/user/SunShineHomes

Website: www.annettelawrence.com

Welcome to Annette's World

For more than 17 years, Annette Lawrence has been selling real estate in the Tampa Bay area. She started out selling commercial real estate and moved to residential sales in 2001. Her focus is on the price point segment that represents 60% of the local market: single-family homes priced at or below $400,000. Her typical buyer is a 30+ couple who is relocating to the area, or second-home buyers who have selected Tampa Bay as their destination.

Realtor Annette Lawrence—from a screen capture of one of her many YouTube videos.

Annette is ardent about what she does. Her real estate philosophy is that home buyers must fall in love with a community before they have the passion to buy; her marketing philosophy is that an overwhelming presence will displace the competition.

Like most realtors, Annette has embraced the Internet as a channel for displaying real estate listings. She maintains several websites, each with a specific purpose: Some are lead capture landing pages, some are informational, and some are for the sole purpose of promoting personal branding and listings. Many of the websites aim to assuage client expectations or to facilitate transaction coordination among the buyer, seller, agent, title company, and lenders. She is always looking for new ways to promote her properties—which ultimately led her to YouTube.

Promoting Real Estate the YouTube Way

Annette got the idea of using YouTube by spending some time with web search engines. She found that the frequency of searches containing the word *video* with a location name greatly exceeded the number containing the words *homes* or *real estate* with the same location. And when you're talking web video, YouTube is the first site that comes to mind.

When doing her research, Annette saw YouTube as a way to promote her properties in a cost- and time-efficient manner. As she puts it, "YouTube offered a desired viral component with streaming and imbed capability that allowed a reasonably easy means to minimize my direct time."

Her first videos were a series of "Refreshing Hikes" that highlighted area attractions, touted benefits of the locale, and promoted the Florida lifestyle. This fit into her overall approach to selling:

My philosophy is to promote my brand via unrelated sources. When my primary message is delivered, the consumer is already aware of my prevalence in my market, my community engagement, and my expansive resources and knowledge of the area. These videos create a familiarity and trust in the consumer prior to actually meeting me.

Thus the majority of Annette's YouTube videos serve much as tour guides to a particular community. Other videos, of course, highlight specific properties, functioning as more direct sales vehicles.

Based on this strategy, some of Annette's videos have attracted more than 20,000 viewers; others might get only 200 views. It all depends on how broad the appeal of the video. As Annette says, "The more localized the video, the lower the viewing count." With that said, the localized videos are often the most significant in attracting solid buyers, which makes them a valuable part of her YouTube mix. Based on the number of viewers, she can project the likelihood of when she will receive a purchase offer.

As of May 2008, Annette has more than 50 videos in her YouTube library. Most are public videos, but she also maintains a library of private videos reserved for potential buyers via invitation. Many of her videos are seasonal, rotating in and out of availability at the appropriate time of year.

These videos have had a dramatic affect on Annette's sales. She credits this to the unique nature of her videos and the quality of the narratives, which distinguish her presentations from those of other realtors. She also believes that the companion high-resolution videos provide a "knock your socks off" immersion every home seller wants to have for their home.

Producing an Effective Real Estate Video

It doesn't take a lot of money to produce one of Annette's real estate videos; a typical five-minute video will cost between $500 and $800 to produce. Even at that, Annette makes sure each video has multiple uses (suitable for multiple applications and websites) before making the investment.

Most of Annette's videos are slideshow-like virtual home tours. They contain dozens of images set to appealing background music, often with audio commentary by Annette or another narrator. Naturally, each video begins and ends with Annette's contact information. They typically run four or five minutes in length.

A typical video home tour, this one of a villa in the Clearwater area.

Each video begins and ends with prominent contact information.

Before she starts work on a new video, Annette does a lot of research on the property for sale and on potential buyers. Here's how she approaches a new project:

First, I need a clue! What would a person be willing to exchange an irreplaceable piece of their life for? I feel an obligation to convey information of use to the viewer, in addition to my messages. When I do a home tour I also include area information and images any visitor, resident, home buyer or home seller would find beneficial.

When it comes time to produce the video, the biggest chore is getting quality source images; this is also the most expensive part of the process. She starts with about 100 images and throws out all those blurry pictures, foot shots, and other unusable pictures. Then it's time for image optimization (editing), cropping, and, if needed, stitching together of multiple images for larger panoramas. She reduces the size of each image to something appropriate for YouTube viewing, and then starts putting the presentation together—sequencing the shots and adding transitions and pans for a "Ken Burns" effect. Next, she applies text overlays to the presentation, creates and records an accompanying narrative, and then synchronizes background clips with image subject segments. With all that done, it's time to render (publish) the video, convert it to a YouTube-friendly format, and post it to YouTube.

Promoting the Videos

Annette has several unique ways in which she promotes her YouTube videos. One I find particularly intriguing involves the seller of a property in the promotion. She encourages the homeowners to send their home's YouTube video link to 5,000 of their closest friends—and have all of them give the video a five-star rating. This helps the video appear higher on viewer search results pages, thus gaining increased exposure for the video.

Another approach is to embed a video of a refreshing hike or recent event into existing websites. As Annette says, "Folks love these videos and will click through to my YouTube videos." She embeds personal message videos into vertical channel sites, providing very specialized information. These sites also host avatars with welcoming messages; the avatar's text-to-speech capability enables her to communicate to hundreds of communities with a single message edit.

To help promote these vertical websites, Annette uses a variety of traditional and new media tools. She says that one of the most effective promotional tools is the old-fashioned road sign. The sign most often contains nothing more than the site's URL, such as www.mydunedin.com (for properties in Dunedin, Florida). In this instance, Annette says that every citizen of Dunedin will check out the site, just to see what it's about!

Advice to Other Businesses

Annette likes the viral nature of the YouTube service, how a video can just take off when discovered by viewers. She's also a big fan of YouTube's new statistics-reporting: "The Insight function provides me the tools I need to generalize where to project my brand in remote locales."

As Annette points out, using YouTube is like any web-based endeavor. You need to understand, in your enterprise, how to fan the consumer into your net. Here's how she puts it:

Now, how will the fellow shivering in his socks in Nebraska (or whoever your subject is) type words that will find your message? As a businessperson, you must know how this takes place. If you believe you can hire someone who knows your business better than you—well, money talks and yours will be saying 'bye-bye.'

Obviously knowing your business is imperative. Knowing how you want to do business is equally important. Some would say my business is real estate. They may also say McDonald's business is hamburgers. Both, of course, are incorrect. My business model is derived from the book, Rich Dad, Poor Dad. *The poor dad was very good at finding work. The rich dad was very good at finding networks. How is your business connected to meaningful global networks, national networks, regional networks, local networks, and grass roots networks? How are you energizing those networks to work for you? Can you get the same results if you just put out a few road signs? A clear picture of a fuzzy concept won't work.*

Annette sums up her YouTube experience with this timeless advice:

Finally, have patience. Believe in your strategy. And don't do anything you can't measure!

Sounds like a plan to me.

Working with YouTube Video Blogs

12

Managing a Video Blog

For many companies, a video blog (a *vlog*) is an essential part of their online marketing mix. If you're new to the scene, a video blog is like a normal text-based blogs, but with all video postings. Instead of writing down your thoughts and comments, you speak them directly into the camera and then post the resulting videos online.

There are many ways to create and maintain a video blog. If your company hosts its own traditional blog, YouTube makes it easy to send any YouTube video to the blog as a blog posting. You can even create a dedicated video blog consisting of nothing but your YouTube videos.

What a Video Blog Is—And Why You Need One

A vlog is a type of blogging in which you communicate via video instead of text. Instead of posting a paragraph or two of text, you post a short (1–3 minute) video.

A post to a video blog doesn't have to be fancy; most posts consist of a single person sitting and talking in front of a video camera or webcam. That doesn't mean you can't create fancier posts; you might, for example, want to post from a remote conference and show off some of the surroundings. But because the goal of a video blog, just like a text-based blog, is fresh content, you get more points for frequent posts than you do for high production values.

If you create a video blog, you don't want to create a few initial posts and then abandon it. Unlike YouTube, where an older video can attract viewers a year or more after its initial posting, a video blog without fresh posts quickly loses viewers. Video blog viewers, like readers of a traditional text-based blog, expect fresh content on a regular basis. You need to post at least once a week, more often as possible, to retain loyal viewers. If you post less frequently, viewers drop your vlog from their syndication or watch lists. If you're not posting, viewers quickly forget you.

note

Although some vlog viewers go directly to your vlog to view posts, most access your vlog by subscribing to a syndication feed, typically via RSS or Atom, and then view your posts in some sort of newsreader program. These syndication feeds notify subscribers when you post new content; if you don't post anything new, there are no notifications sent.

The goal of a video blog is to distribute your message on a regular basis to those interested parties who prefer to obtain their information visually. Some people, you see, prefer to absorb information visually. Give them all the text you want, but they want to watch a video instead. We are, after all, becoming a society of viewers, not readers. Instead of burdening these customers with long text posts, you insert your message into a continuing series of short videos.

Over time, the posts to your video blog combine to create a library of video information—almost like a visual FAQ for your company. Thus the vlog becomes more important as important information is cataloged, available for reference by future viewers.

tip

Your video blog posts can also be thought of as video podcasts—video versions of the traditional audio podcast. With this in mind, you can register your vlog posts with podcasting distribution and syndication services, such as Apple's iTunes.

Creating and Maintaining a Video Blog

How do you create a video blog? It's just like creating a traditional text-based blog, but with video posts instead of text posts.

Creating the Vlog

You don't need a special video host for your vlog; any traditional blog host can do the job. You can either host the vlog on your company's website or have it hosted by one of the many blog-hosting communities, such as Blogger or WordPress (www.wordpress.com).

In terms of look and feel, your blog needs to resemble your company's official website. Naturally, you want to embellish the listing of posts with useful information in the margins, such as links to your company's official website, new product announcements, contact information, and the like. Just remember, your video blog isn't an isolated vehicle; it's an important and coordinated part of your overall online marketing mix.

This is what I've done with my Video Blogging for Business blog (businessvideoblog.blogspot.com), shown in Figure 12.1. Every time I upload a new video to YouTube, I also post it to this blog. As long as you keep the blog current with new videos, viewers keep coming back to find out the latest news and announcements.

FIGURE 12.1

A blog full of videos—the author's Video Blogging for Business blog.

Creating Vlog Posts

As you might surmise, you can create a video blog post using any type of video equipment. Many creators of personal video blogs record them via webcam; webcam video is low cost and easy to produce. For your business video blog, you probably want slightly higher production values, which you can get using a standard consumer-grade camcorder and a tripod.

However you shoot your video blog posts, here are some tips to keep in mind for most-effective results:

- **Watch the lighting**—Many personal vlogs are notable for their lack of viewability; they look as if they were shot in a darkened bedroom (and, in fact, might have been). Whether you use a webcam or camcorder, you need to make sure the subject is getting sufficient light to look good on the web page. Although this can be accomplished with carefully managed existing lighting, you'll probably get better results from some sort of supplemental lighting—either a camcorder-mounted light or a couple of freestanding photofloods or strobe lights. The better the lighting, the better the subject looks.

- **Get close, but not too close**—How should the subject appear in the shot? If the subject is too far away (close to a full body shot), he looks too small, and you can't see his lips move. Get him too close to the camera and you can see every pore on his face. Better to shoot from the waist up, perhaps from the middle of chest up. As you can see in Figure 12.2, this positions the subject full in the frame, big enough to work in a small video window but not so big that you see nothing but face. (And don't chop off the top of the subject's head in the shot!)

- **Dress appropriately**—A personal video blogger might be able to get away with wearing an old T-shirt on camera, but a business vlogger needs to look more professional. Depending on the type of image you want to convey, that might mean wearing a polo shirt, button-down shirt, or even a suit and tie. Keep the colors muted (no screaming colors) and the design simple (no busy patterns). The speaker's face, not his clothing, should draw the viewer's attention.

- **Use a plain background**—Similarly, don't let a busy background distract from the person on-camera. Situate the subject in front of a plain white or light gray background—or, for a special effect, in front of a solid black background. Avoid patterns and bright colors that draw attention to themselves.

FIGURE 12.2

The best way to frame a video blog post—from the middle of the chest up.

- **Use a script, or not**—Some vloggers like to prepare their remarks, which is fine as long as they make it appear as if they're speaking extemporaneously. However, know that most viewers expect a vlog (like a traditional blog) to be personal and direct, which argues for speaking off-the-cuff, if you can. If you decide to record without a script, be prepared for multiple takes; it often takes several tries to get everything exactly right.

- **Listen to the sound**—The audio of your video blog can be a problem if you're using a low-cost webcam; most webcams of this nature have rather ineffectual built-in microphones. For clarity's sake, you get better results using a camcorder that accepts an external microphone. Turn off the internal mic and put a lavaliere mic on the speaker, and you notice a world of difference.

- **Keep it short**—Above all, remember that a video blog post is a *short* musing, not a long dissertation. Viewers don't want to sit through 10 minutes of boring lecture. It's better to keep your comments short (less than 3 minutes) and, if possible, light. You want to keep people watching, not have them turn you off midway through your post.

Follow this advice and you can create appealing video posts, which is the best way to attract viewers to your vlog.

Adding YouTube Videos to Your Blog or Vlog

If you already have a blog (traditional or video), YouTube lets you post any or all of your YouTube videos to that blog. This is the easiest way to create a video blog—just add video to what already exists.

Configuring YouTube for Your Blog

Before you post a video to your blog, you have to tell YouTube about the blog. Otherwise, YouTube won't know where to send the post.

Start by clicking the Account link at the top of any YouTube page; when the My Account page appears, scroll down to the Account section and click the Blog Posting Settings link. This displays the page shown in Figure 12.3; click the Add a Blog/Site button.

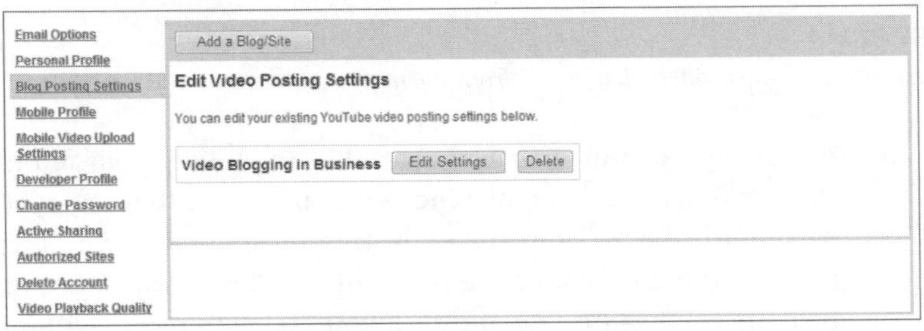

FIGURE 12.3

Getting ready to configure YouTube for your own personal blog.

> **note**
>
> YouTube supports automatic posting to the following blog hosts: Blogger, FreeWebs, Friendster, LiveJournal, Piczo, WordPress.com, and WordPress self-hosted blogs.

YouTube now displays the Add a Blog/Site page shown in Figure 12.4. Pull down the Blog Service list and select your blog host; then enter your blog username and password. Click the Add Blog button, and you're finished with the preliminary setup.

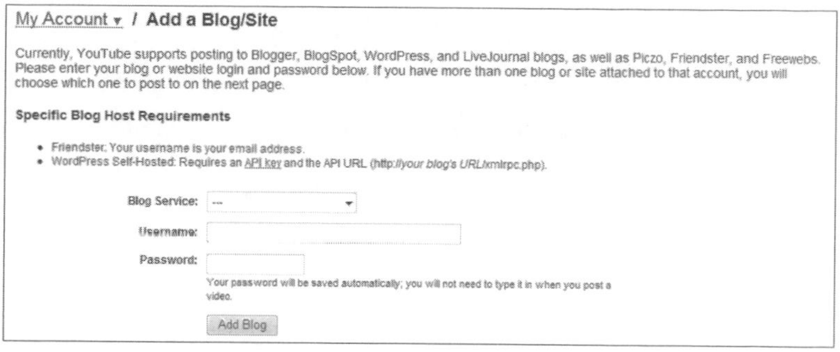

FIGURE 12.4

Adding a blog to your YouTube configuration.

tip

If you have multiple blogs, repeat this setup procedure for each blog you post to. You can manage all the blogs you add from the Edit Video Settings page.

Posting a Video to Your Blog

After you configure YouTube, it's a snap to send any public YouTube video to your blog. Just open the video page, scroll to the options box below the video player window, and click the Share tab. Click the More Share Option link and this section expands to include blog posting options, as shown in Figure 12.5.

Go to the Post to a Blog section and then pull down the Blog list; select the blog you want to post to. Enter a title for the post and then enter any text you want to accompany the video. Click the Post to Blog button, and YouTube posts the video (and accompanying text) to your blog as a new post, like the one shown in Figure 12.6.

tip

If you have a WordPress blog, you can also embed a YouTube video into your blog using the following code: [youtube=*url*]. Replace *url* with the video's URL, as copied from the video page, and the click-to-play video will be embedded.

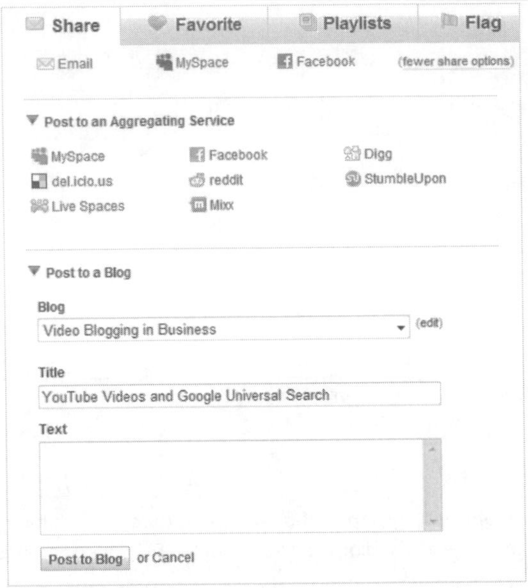

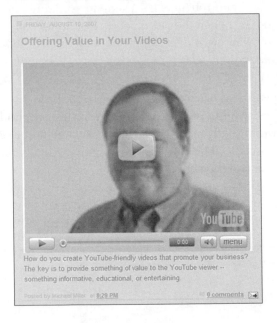

FIGURE 12.5
Preparing to post a YouTube video to your blog.

FIGURE 12.6
A YouTube video appearing as a Blogger blog post.

Managing Your Video Blog

When you produce a series of vlog posts over an extended period of time, you have to deal with managing the continuing content of your video blog. A vlog, like a traditional text blog, is a living thing; new content is posted; old content rolls off into the archives.

Whereas some might recommended deleting older posts after a period of time, that's not an approach I personally take. Assuming that there's nothing incorrect, outdated, or embarrassing in your older posts, there's no reason not to leave them up; what's old to you might be new to someone else. And the more posts you have online, the more potential viewers you can attract.

That said, you may want to delete old videos if they no longer fit your mission or match your current branding or look and feel. For example, if your company changes its product mixes, there is little value of keeping videos online that push a product you no longer sell. Same thing with the look and feel; if you've polished your production values and now shoot everything on a high-tech set, you might not want to retain those videos shot with a handheld camera in your building's parking lot.

Those videos you do leave online eventually move into your vlog archives. As with the blogs you manage, old vlog posts scroll off the main page and are typically accessed via a link to the month they were posted. You can improve access to archived videos by tagging those videos up front and including a list of tags in the sidebar of your vlog. This way viewers can browse or search for specific older content in which they're interested.

tip

Should you maintain a consistency of look over time? Although there are differing opinions, I say yes—to a point. I recommend using a consistent background for most of your posts (unless you're shooting in the field) to establish a look and feel with your viewers. Also, try to wear a consistent type of clothing (don't mix a T-shirt in one post with a suit and tie in another), although it's certainly okay to change outfits from post to post.

The Big Picture

Blogs are an important part of any company's online marketing mix. To that end, you can include your YouTube videos in your blog as individual blog posts; YouTube makes the posting process relatively painless.

You can also create a separate video blog consisting of nothing but your uploaded videos. This is a great way to communicate with those customers who prefer watching to reading—as well as to consolidate all your videos into one easy-to-navigate website. ■

13

Integrating Text Blogs and Video Blogs

In the previous chapter, you learned how to create a video blog (*vlog*); it's relatively easy to use your YouTube videos as vlog posts. But a video blog is only part of your online marketing mix. A successful business needs to integrate text blogs, video blogs, and audio podcasts as well as other media components.

What role should a video blog play in your online marketing mix? That's entirely up to you, of course, but you might want to follow some guidelines. Read on to learn more.

Communicating with Your Customers Online

Traditional advertising in print or on radio or television is a one-way communication. Your ad broadcasts your message to potential customers, but your customers have no way of communicating back to you. (Short of buying your product, of course, but that's an indirect, if welcome, message.)

One of the key advantages of the Internet as a marketing medium is that it allows for two-way communications. Instead of talking *to* your customers, you can now talk *with* them. This is especially true with blogs and vlogs.

When you create a blog or vlog post, you initiate a conversation. The replies to your post are your customers talking back to you, and one of the best ways to increase customer loyalty is to engage them in this sort of ongoing communication. With each post you make, you're forging a tighter bond with your most important customers.

For this reason, most companies today, large or small, view a blog as an essential part of their marketing mix. Consider a video blog as a similar way to communicate with your customers online. You initiate the conversation by recording and posting your video musings and then encourage feedback from viewers either via text comments or through responding video posts—both of which YouTube enables your viewers to do.

The replies to your blog and vlog posts are what matter. By reading your customers' responses to your posts, you get an insight into what's on their minds—what matters to them. Over time, your blog/vlog readers drive your posts, and you hone your message for your entire customer base.

This is why any company that is not blogging or vlogging is at a competitive disadvantage. A company that talks only to its customers but doesn't listen to them is left behind in this new online marketplace. If you encourage two-way communication via your blog/vlog, you're more in touch with your customer base, and you can tune your products and services to meet their needs. In other words, blogging/vlogging is a great market research tool that appears only to a promotional device.

Your People Are Your Message

Blogs and vlogs also enable you to add nuance to the message your company communicates. Instead of a single, monolithic company voice, your blog and vlog can include posts from employees throughout your organization. Your company becomes personalized and easier to identify with.

This is especially true with video blogs, where customers can see and hear the people behind the posts. Even if only your CEO posts, your customers can better identify with a living, breathing human being than with an impersonal advertising message. It's even better to have posts by multiple employees, from throughout your organization, so that your company has multiple faces.

It's like that old saying—people don't buy from companies, they buy from people. The more you can present your people as the face of your company, the more your customers can identify with them and your company. Videos let you put real, honest-to-goodness human beings front and center better than any other medium. You should take advantage of this facet of online marketing.

There's another reason to have multiple individuals posting from within your organization. Each employee has his or her own unique interests, opinions, and voice. Any three employees talking about the same topic present it in three unique ways. One person's approach might appeal to part of your customer base; another person might appeal to a completely different customer base. The more employees you have talking, the more types of customers you can attract.

In addition, you can engage different employees to talk about different topics. Let them speak about something they're passionate about—create an army of topic-specific experts. This approach reaches the broadest number of potential customers online.

caution

One of the biggest mistakes companies make is to appoint a senior executive as the single face of the company in their blogs and vlogs. Even the most naive consumer quickly realizes that someone else writes the posts—that the executive doesn't even answer his own email. It's better to create posts by employees more directly in touch with the customer base.

Expanding Your Message Across the Web

The two-way communication enabled by blogs and vlogs (and, to a lesser extent, audio podcasts) can take place only when customers find your site. How, then, can you publicize your blog/vlog and spread your message across a wider swath of the Internet? Here are some approaches that others have found effective.

Syndicate!

One of the key way to disseminate your blog and vlog posts is to syndicate your site content via a site feed. A *feed* is an automatically updated stream of a blog's contents, enabled by a special XML (*Extensible Markup Language*) file format called RSS (*Really Simple Syndication*). A blog that has an RSS feed enabled automatically publishes any updated content as a special XML file that contains the RSS feed. The syndicated feed is then normally picked up by RSS feed reader programs and RSS aggregators for websites; Google indexes the feeds as part of its Blog Search function.

When you enable your blog/vlog for syndication, any user subscribing to your site automatically receives any new post you make. In effect, your site pushes your new content to interested subscribers, without them having to revisit your site to find out what's new. The more subscribers you have, the more interested readers or viewers you have.

For this reason, you want to enable your blog/vlog for both RSS and Atom syndication. Most blog-hosting services make this easy to do, typically by adding an RSS Feed or Subscribe button somewhere in the margins of the blog. When users click the button, they initiate the process of subscribing; this might involve copying some XML code into their feed reader program or choosing which feed readers they want to use to track your postings. The process is simpler than it sounds, especially because many personalized home pages (such as iGoogle and My Yahoo!) can now track blog syndication as part of their content modules.

> **note**
>
> Atom is a feed format similar to RSS, with a few extra features. You should make your blog/vlog compatible with both RSS and Atom feeds.

Link!

Another way to get your blog/vlog known across the Web is to make sure other sites link to it. This happens naturally if you have a truly content-rich site; if you build a blog/vlog that contains tons of useful information, word gets out...eventually.

You can speed up the process, however, by finding other sites to link back to your site. This is a time-consuming manual process, I'm afraid; you have to email each site you want to link to you and ask the webmaster to do so. Some sites do so if asked (and if your site is important to their visitors); some sites create a reciprocal link, if you also link to them; some sites link to you if you pay them to do so; and some sites won't link back to you, no matter what. It's a bit of a crapshoot.

If this sounds too daunting, you can employ a link management service to do this link hunting for you. Just Google for "link management" or "link building" and take a look at what comes up in the results.

> **caution**
>
> Beware any firm that promises you a set number of links to your site. Nobody can know in advance how many links they can build until they start trying!

Promote!

When trying to broaden the audience for your blog, don't neglect good old-fashioned promotion. This could include all or any of the following, plus anything else you can come up with:

- Prominent mention on your official company website
- Mention in your company's traditional print, radio, and television advertisements
- Mention in your company's press releases, as well as a dedicated press release mentioning the launch of your blog/vlog
- An email marketing mailing promoting the blog/vlog
- Mention of your vlog in the text accompanying all your YouTube videos—and, perhaps, an onscreen mention of your vlog's URL within each video
- A contest (conducted in other media) to draw visitors to your blog/vlog
- A concerted PR effort to get mention of your blog/vlog in related blogs

In other words, use your accumulated marketing prowess to uncover ways to let potential customers know about your blog or vlog—either on the Internet or off!

Be Social!

You can also spread the word of your blog/vlog by making your site more social. That means adding buttons for social bookmark and social news-sharing sites, such as Digg (www.digg.com) and Reddit (www.reddit.com). Visitors use these sites to share sites and pages of interest with other people.

You can also publish your blog/vlog to social news sites. These are category-specific sites that attract communities of like-minded individuals who consume news related to the topic at hand. Users of these sites can comment on your blog and vlog postings; if a lot of people vote on a story, it can hit the site's home page and drive a lot of traffic back to your blog/vlog.

An added benefit of a bookmark to your blog/vlog on a social site is that each bookmark creates a new link back to your site. And, as most savvy webmasters know, your ranking in Google and Yahoo! search results is at least partly dependent on the number of pages that link to your site. The more bookmarks, the more links—and the higher your search results.

Make Your Blog/Vlog Search Friendly

Many visitors find blogs/vlogs by searching for related content; if your blog or vlog postings appear prominently in Google and Yahoo! search results, it attracts a lot of new customers to your site. The key, then, is optimizing your blog/vlog for these search engines. How do you do this?

Blog optimization is a lot like traditional website optimization. The first thing to pay attention to is your blog's *template*—the content that surrounds the blog posts themselves. Your template needs to include keywords within the text that reference the main topics of the blog, preferably high on the page. You should also place keywords in the template's <title> tag and in all alternative image text. Search engines look for these keywords when they're indexing web pages; the more frequent, more prominent, and more relevant the keywords in your blog, the higher your site appears in the search engine's results.

You can also optimize each blog post for search engine indexing. For this reason, it's important to include keywords in the title of each post; because many syndicators/aggregators list only the title of a post, this makes the title much more important than the main text of a post. You should make the title a link so that the search engines pick up the link from the title to the post.

Post Your Videos on Multiple Sites

Finally, here's one that you might not have thought of. The more sites on which your videos appear, the more opportunities you have for inclusion in Google and Yahoo! search results. If your video is embedded on three different sites, you could get three different places on the search results page—all for the same video!

So, where can you post your video? You can post it on your video blog, of course, but also on your traditional blog, on your company's official website, and on YouTube. Also, you should enable the embedding feature on YouTube to encourage interested viewers to embed your video on their websites and blogs. The more places your video appears, the more viewers you have!

What Makes a Good Video Blog?

With all this talk of creating and promoting your video blog, it's critical that your vlog be as appealing as possible to attract the highest number of viewers. Just how do you go about making a good video blog?

First, realize that a good video blog is just like a good text-based blog: It's engaging, relevant, timely, and personal. It's a two-way communication between the people of your organization and your customers. It's not an overt commercial.

You make a video blog good by thinking about your customers—not about your company. This isn't (solely) about your company, your brand, your products, or your senior management team. It's about what's important to your current and potential customers.

A good vlog isn't just talk. It's also about action and giving your customers what they want in information, education, and entertainment. You have to provide real value in terms of what matters to your customers.

> **tip**
>
> A good vlog, like a good blog, has to be transparent. You can't pretend to be something you're not; your vlog has to reflect your company's culture and present what your company is all about.

The way to get smart about making a better vlog is simple: Spend time in the community. That means diving head-first into other online blogs and forums frequented by your customer base. Find out what they're talking about; what they like and dislike; how they talk, and why they talk, and when they talk. Get to know what's going on so that you can better integrate your vlog into this community.

Here's something else you need to know upfront: It's going to take a lot more time than you thought. You have to make a lot of posts, and each post takes time to shoot, edit, and upload. In addition, you need to monitor and respond to all the comments left on your vlog. Your vlog, like a text-based blog, is a living thing that requires constant attention. You have to be prepared to keep it fresh and functioning.

Managing a Multiple-Channel Online Marketing Mix

As noted earlier in this chapter, your video blog is just one component of your online marketing mix. Vlogs, blogs, social networks, search advertising, banner advertising, public relations—they're all important. How do you manage all these diverse yet interrelated components?

First, realize that no matter how many different elements you're managing, they all have to present the same cohesive image and message to the customer. Don't think that your customers know of only a single element; they see more than one thing you're doing, and the different pieces can't be cognitively dissonant. What one element says, the others should reinforce.

With that said, you need to play to the strengths of each component. A banner ad is best for presenting a simple, bold image to a mass audience; a blog is best for encouraging two-way communication with individual consumers. Know how to use each component of the mix to best effect, and don't try to make any single element do what it can't do.

You should also recognize how different elements affect each other. For example, the popularity of a blog or of your online videos can help to drive up the ranking of your search results; thus these (and other) elements affect the success of your search engine marketing. Learn how to drive customers from your mass market advertising to your more targeted blogs and email marketing. Make each element work on its own and with other elements.

> **tip**
>
> Your online marketing plan doesn't have to be limited to a single vlog. You can create multiple vlogs, each dedicated to a specific topic, which may be a better way to target specific customer or product segments.

Converting Viewers to Paying Customers

Now we come to the hundred-dollar question: How do you convert a customer from being a passive vlog viewer to a paying customer? Here is where your vlog page design comes to the fore. You have to forget what you think you know a vlog or blog has to look like. In reality, a blog/vlog can look almost like a traditional web page. There's no reason you can't list your specials of the week in the margin, put a link to a product page at the top, or even display a banner ad for your other website at the bottom. The key is to include some sort of conversion mechanism in your vlog's template to drive traffic from the vlog to your action-oriented website.

That's right, your blog or vlog is only the first step to customer conversion. In reality, it functions like an advertisement in that it attracts eyeballs; your job is to transfer those eyeballs to a page or site that contains a direct call to action. The success of your presentation is not (just) about the information contained in your blog/vlog, it's also about what people can do with that information. Your ultimate call to action has to tell visitors how they can buy what they've been viewing, reading about, or discussing. It is, at the end of the day, all about the sales.

---

note

Discover specific ways to make money from your vlog postings and other online videos in Chapter 16, "Generating Revenues from Your YouTube Videos."

The Big Picture

A video blog is just one part of your company's online marketing mix. As such, it needs to integrate with and reinforce the other components of the mix in presenting a consistent image and message. At the same time, it has to emphasize its unique capabilities to communicate directly with your customer base.

A good vlog is just like a good blog; it's a forum for two-way interaction with your most devoted customers. Ultimately, you don't use your vlog to talk *to* your customers; you use it to talk *with* your customers. This communication isn't from a faceless corporate entity, but rather from the living, breathing human beings who make up your employee base. Videos, after all, let you present real people to your viewers; they let you put a personal face on your company, brand, and products. ∎

Profile: Stone Brewing Company

Company Profile

> **Company:** Stone Brewing Company
>
> **Product:** Beer
>
> **YouTube channel:** www.youtube.com/user/StoneBrewingCo
>
> **Website:** www.stonebrew.com

Welcome to the World of Stone Brewing Company

The Stone Brewing Company is a microbrewery based in Escondido, California, just north of San Diego. Beer lovers Greg Koch and Steve Wagner first met in 1989, when Steve's band was using rehearsal space at Greg's music studios. They ran into each other again a few years later when both men took a Sensory Evaluation of Beer class at UC Davis. Eventually they decided to open their own brewery and did so in 1996.

The Stone brewery has a capacity of 70,000 barrels per year and includes an onsite bottling line. The brewery is also home to the Stone Brewing World Bistro & Gardens, a 300-seat restaurant with a large outdoor patio and an acre of gardens.

The company brews a variety of popular beers, including Stone Pale Ale, Stone Smoked Porter, Stone IPA, Arrogant Bastard Ale, and a variety of special releases. You can find Stone beers throughout the Southern California region and in select markets throughout the United States. (Although not in my new home state of Minnesota—darn it!)

Some of the fine beers brewed by the Stone Brewing Company.

Promoting the Company via a Video Blog

Promoting a small brewery is a difficult challenge; it obviously doesn't have the budget of its larger competitors. To meet this challenge, Stone CEO Greg Koch came up with the idea of a video blog (a **vlog**), posted on the company's website and on YouTube. Why a video blog? Here's how Greg remembers the genesis:

There was so much going on in the world of Stone at the time...especially with the beginning of the construction of our new brewery. I really wanted to capture it to be able to share with all the fans of Stone, to take them on the journey with us. And for posterity.

Each vlog entry runs from 2 to 20 minutes. The postings focus on Stone Brewing happenings, news, and announcements, all from Greg's personal perspective. These vlog postings enable a unique bond between customer and company because you're hearing about Stone Brewing from a company insider, completely unfiltered.

Greg's video log resides on both the Stone Brewing website and on YouTube. The resolution of the videos is a little higher on the Stone site, but, as Greg says, YouTube is more universal. To date, he has posted close to 300 videos; he posts at least one video per month, sometimes as often as once a week.

Some of Stone Brewing's many video blog entries.

Has the video blog affected Stone's sales? Greg isn't sure. As he puts it, "They are not commercials in even the loosest sense. They are not intended to do anything other than to share an insider's view—specifically from my perspective—into the world of Stone Brewing."

Stone's videos get decent viewership on YouTube and on Stone's own website. It's a low-cost way to reach out and touch the company's customers—and put a human face on the corporation.

The Making of a Video Blog

How low cost is Stone Brewing's video blog? When I asked Greg how much they spend to produce a typical video, his reply was, "Not a dime." And he means it. He shoots all the videos himself—the on-camera person, the interviewer, and the cameraman, all at the same time. Here's how he does it:

Ninety-nine percent of the videos are shot while I hold the camera at arm's length. I don't use the viewfinder at all, and as such I am able to simply take the viewer with me in the conversation (some of which is admittedly not perfectly framed!). I then cut the clips together in chronological order. I do not add any effects or voiceovers.

That's a low-cost approach to creating online videos, but for Stone Brewing it works. Greg's videos are uniquely personal; the "arm's length" perspective brings the viewer face-to-face with Greg, and when he turns the camera around, the viewer sees what he sees. It's just like being there!

An "arm's length" video blog posting from Greg Koch, Stone Brewing CEO.

Advice to Other Businesses

A video blog with frequent postings is a great way to reach out to a company's most dedicated customers. As Greg notes about his own vlog viewers:

We like to keep people informed and clued in, to the degree that they want to be. The type of person who enjoys Stone beers tends to be the type of person that is more inquisitive than average. They are seekers of culture and information.

And they watch his vlog to keep up-to-date with what the company and its founder are up to.

Interestingly, Stone Brewing's most viewed blog posting had little to do with brewing. When he posted a video about the 2007 San Diego wildfires, viewership spiked. Greg says, "Many people responded that my short video gave them a better sense of what [the fire] was like than any of the voluminous TV pieces."

That's the power of a video blog: to bring viewers personally into the picture, to make them feel as if they were there.

Promotion and Monetization

14

Tracking Performance

Posting a video to YouTube is just the start of the marketing process. You need to judge how effective that video is—how many viewers it attracts and how many sales result from those viewers.

Fortunately, YouTube provides a number of metrics you can use to track the performance of each video you post. Read on to learn more.

Why Tracking Is Important

Why should you bother tracking the performance of your YouTube videos? For the same reasons you track the performance of other parts of your marketing mix—to fine-tune your activities to have bigger impact, to measure the effectiveness of your efforts, and to learn from your efforts when planning future activities.

Let's look at each reason individually.

Fine-Tuning Your Efforts

You don't have to wait until the end of a campaign to track its performance. In fact, it's a good idea to look at what's happening while it's happening so that you can make any mid-course corrections that might be necessary.

Let's say, for example, that you launch a series of YouTube videos but discover, after the first few weeks, that viewership is much less than what you anticipated. Why is this? What do you do about it?

Can you tweak upcoming videos to make them more attractive to potential viewers? These are all questions you can answer *now*, without having to wait until the end of the campaign. Track the performance and make necessary changes along the way—this is how you get the most out of any marketing campaign.

Measuring Effectiveness

At the conclusion of the campaign, you need to measure just how effective it was. Did the campaign meet your goals? Did you achieve the viewership you wanted? Was there the expected increase in sales? And if not, why not?

You need to apply the same sort of scrutiny to your YouTube activities as you do to any marketing campaign. That means setting goals beforehand, and then measuring the actual performance against those goals. Just as important, you need to analyze the results to see why your videos under- or over-performed against expectations. Set a goal, measure performance, and then analyze that performance—that's Marketing 101.

Planning Future Activities

Finally, you need to learn from your YouTube activities. If your first campaign bombed, figure out why and apply that knowledge to your next campaign. If the campaign was a success, determine what contributed to that success, so you can replicate it in future efforts. Each activity you engage in should be a learning experience that informs the next activity, and the one after that. Don't repeat your mistakes—and don't abandon your successes.

Tracking Basic Viewership

Fortunately, YouTube makes tracking basic metrics somewhat easy, thanks to several online tracking tools. You use these tools to track viewership of your videos, as well as reveal other important statistics.

YouTube's first tool for tracking the performance of a video is located right on the page for each video, on the Statistics & Data tab just below the video player. When you click this tab, you see a variety of statistics, as shown in Figure 14.1.

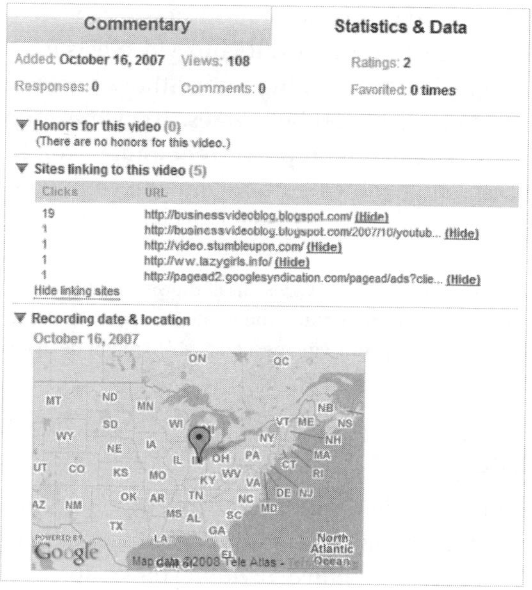

FIGURE 14.1

Tracking viewership on the Statistics & Data tab of a video page.

The provided statistics and information include

- **Views**—The total number of times the video has been viewed
- **Ratings**—The number of users who have rated the video
- **Responses**—The number of video responses left for this video
- **Comments**—The number of text comments left about this video
- **Favorites**—The number of users who have added this video to their favorites list
- Honors for this video
- Sites linking to this video
- Recording date and location

The Statistics & Data tab gives you a quick look at how this video is performing. Particularly useful is the Views metric, which tells you precisely how many times the video has been watched. I also like the list of sites that link back to the video, which includes a count of the actual clicks made from that site to your video on the YouTube site.

When it comes to judging performance, how many views is a good number? That's hard to say. Certainly, if your video gets a million views overnight, you're doing something right—that's pure viral status. But for particular types of videos and businesses, 100 views might be good (for example, if you're selling high-priced real estate). You have to judge performance based on your own parameters and with realistic expectations.

tip

It's particularly useful to compare views for all the videos in your library. Although raw numbers might not tell you much, comparative numbers tell you which of your videos are performing best and which might need replaced.

Gaining Insight

If you want more detailed performance metrics, you can turn to YouTube's newest analytical tool, dubbed Insight. The Insight tool enables you to view detailed statistics about each video you've uploaded. You can drill down through the data to view activity by geographic region over selected periods; you can even compare the popularity of your video to other videos in that region.

To access the Insight tool, click Account, My Videos to display your entire list of uploaded videos. Next to each video, as you can see in Figure 14.2, is an Insight button; click it to display the Insight page.

FIGURE 14.2

Click the Insight button to analyze a video's performance.

The Insight page for each video includes three tabs: Views, Popularity, and Discovery. Each tab displays a particular type of information, as discussed next.

Insight Views

The Views tab, shown in Figure 14.3, presents a graphical display of the number of views for your video, both over time and by region.

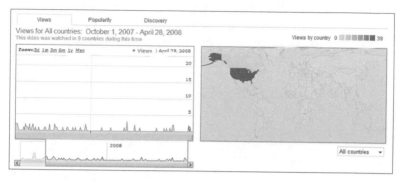

FIGURE 14.3

Using the Views tab to analyze the view count for a video by time and region.

The left graph displays the number of views over the designated period. You can expand or contract the graph to show views for the past 5 days, 1 month, 3 months, 6 months, 1 year, or total video life (Max). After you choose a length, you can use the slider beneath the graph to show performance for other periods in the life of the video.

note

YouTube's view count data includes views of the video on the YouTube site as well as views from other sites that embed the video.

The right graph is a map of the world, with the number of views for your video displayed in different colors for each region. To select a specific country, click that country on the map. To select a larger region, select that region from the pull-down list beneath the graph.

note

Insight analyzes performance for the following regions: U.S.A., Asia, Africa, Europe, Middle East, and South America.

When you select a country or region, the view count for that area appears in the left graph. You can return that graph to a combined worldview by clicking the Back to All Countries link.

Insight Popularity

When you want to compare the popularity of your video with other videos in a given country or region, go to the Popularity tab. As you can see in Figure 14.4, this tab has a two-graph display similar to that on the Views tab. What differs is that the left graph charts the popularity of the video as compared to other videos in the selected region or country.

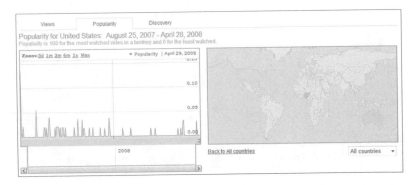

FIGURE 14.4
Using the Popularity tab to compare the popularity of a video with other videos in the selected region.

In this instance, a popularity index measures the video's popularity; the index is like the percentile rankings you find in standard test scores. In this scheme, the most watched video has a ranking of 100, whereas the least watched video has a ranking of 0.

For example, a video with a popularity index of 50 is more popular than 50% of the videos in that region, and a video with an index of 75 is more popular than 75% of other videos. Few videos achieve this type of index score, however; your video is more likely to have an index ranking in the single digits or below.

As with the Views tab, you can view the popularity index by specific time frame (5 days, 1 month, 3 months, and so on) and by specific country or region. Select the time frame in the left graph and the country/region in the map on the right.

note

On the Popularity map, the country where the video is most popular is dark green, whereas the country where it's least popular is light green.

Insight Discovery

Insight's Discovery tab, shown in Figure 14.5, tells you how viewers discovered your video. This is a great way to determine where to put your promotional efforts.

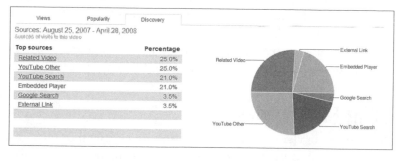

| Views | Popularity | Discovery |

Sources: August 25, 2007 - April 28, 2008
Sources of visits to this video

Top sources	Percentage
Related Video	25.0%
YouTube Other	25.0%
YouTube Search	21.0%
Embedded Player	21.0%
Google Search	3.5%
External Link	3.5%

FIGURE 14.5

Using the Discovery tab to determine how viewers are finding your videos.

The table on the left lists the top sources where your video was discovered. These methods include the following:

- Related videos
- YouTube search
- Embedded players (your video embedded on other sites)
- Google search
- Other links on the YouTube site

The pie chart on the right displays the discovery methods visually. This makes it easier to compare each discovery method, on a percentage basis.

Click a particular discovery method in the table or the pie chart, and you see a list of specific items related to that method. For example, if you click the YouTube Search link, you receive a list of the top search queries that found your video; further click a query link to see all the results for that query, and where your video appears on the results list.

I think the Insight Discovery tool is the most important one in the entire toolkit. It's key in determining how viewers find your videos; until you know this information, it's impossible to determine how to promote your YouTube videos. For example, if you find that the majority of viewers discover a video by searching on Google, you know that you need to optimize future videos for Google search. In this instance, you're further empowered by Insight's listing of what keywords your viewers searched for. With this knowledge in hand, you can make sure to include the most popular keywords in the descriptions of subsequent YouTube videos.

Alternatively, you can use the Discovery tool to determine why a particular video performs less well than others. Look at how viewers did (or, more important, didn't) find a less-viewed video, and you'll find out areas where you need to improve. If, for example, a video didn't pull well via Google search, you know that you need to pay more attention to keywords in future video descriptions. The key is to determine how viewers find out about your videos and then exploit that information.

Tracking Effectiveness

The number of views a video obtains isn't necessarily indicative of how effective it is. A video might gain huge viewership but result in few sales or little brand awareness; conversely, a video with a small number of viewers might result in much higher sales or brand awareness.

Tracking the effectiveness of a video is more difficult than tracking simple viewership. No analytical tools measure this metric; in fact, it's more of a black art than it is a science. With that caveat, there are ways to get a general handle on how effective a video is.

Tracking Interactivity

One measure of effectiveness is how well the video involves the viewers—that is, how viewers interact with the video. You can deduce the level of interaction from the number of comments and video responses left by viewers. The more that the video draws in viewers, the more viewers leave personal comments and responses.

Think of it this way. If your video is just light entertainment, viewers will likely not be inspired to leave comments. If, on the other hand, your video proves particularly useful or educational, viewers are more likely to leave comments to that effect. The more comments you get, the better the video is at involving the viewer.

On a meta level, you can track the effectiveness of all your videos in total by noting the number of subscribers you get to your YouTube channel. If your videos connect with viewers, they're more likely to subscribe to your channel to get notice of future videos. If your videos are less effective, viewers are less likely to subscribe.

Tracking Traffic

If you're using your YouTube videos to sell products or services directly from your website, the best way to measure the effectiveness of each video is simply to track traffic from each YouTube video back to your site. There are a number of ways to do this.

Most website-hosting services provide their own traffic analysis tools. You can also use a third-party tool, such as Blizzard Tracker (www. blizzardtracker.com), GoStats (www.gostats.com), and Opentracker (www. opentracker.net). Also good is Google's own Google Analytics tool (www.google.com/analytics/), shown in Figure 14.6; it is a robust and totally free analysis tool that any website can use.

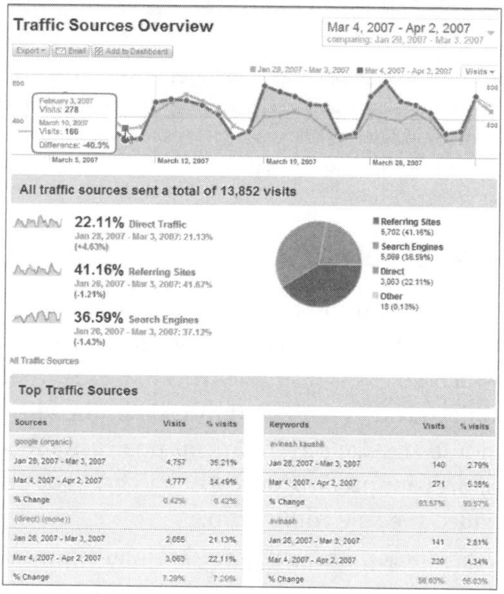

FIGURE 14.6

Using Google Analytics or a similar tool to analyze your website's incoming traffic.

Just about any website analysis tool will show where your site traffic comes from—that is, the previous sites viewed by your site's visitors. By using this type of tool, it's easy enough to track the traffic from the YouTube site (www.youtube.com) to your site. If you see a spike in traffic from YouTube after you post a new video, it's a good bet that the traffic was driven by that video.

More sophisticated website analysis tools track traffic from specific pages on the originating site. This makes it even easier to determine which videos are driving the most traffic back to your site.

Alternatively, you can include a special code for each video you upload to YouTube. The easiest way to do this is to display a unique URL for your main site in each YouTube video; the URL should lead to a unique landing page on your website. For example, you might create a series of landing pages for each of your videos, with URLs such as www.yourwebsite.com/youtubepromo01/, www.yourwebsite.com/youtubepromo02/, www.yourwebsite.com/youtubepromo03/, and so on. This makes it easy to track hits on each specific landing page, providing a detailed analysis of the effectiveness of each originating video.

tip

If you upload videos to multiple video-sharing sites, several services can help you both upload your videos and track each site's relative performance. The most popular of these video syndication/analysis services includes TubeMogul (www.tubemogul.com) and Vidmetrix (www.vidmetrix.com).

Tracking Direct Sales

Ultimately, the best measure of a video's effectiveness is how many sales directly result from the viewing of that video. Determining which sales result from which videos is a simple tracking issue. Assign each video a special tracking code and include that code in the video's text description and onscreen information screen. Encourage customers to enter that tracking code on your product purchase or checkout page, and you know from which video the sale came from.

What's a good conversion rate? That's entirely within your judgment; for some companies, converting 1 sale per 100 views is good performance, whereas other companies might be satisfied with a 1 in 10,000 conversion rate. It all depends on the type of product you sell.

In any instance, the total number of conversions might be less important than comparing the conversion rates of different videos. If one video has a 0.1% conversion rate and another a 0.5% rate, you know that second video is five times more effective than the first one. Knowing that, you can then analyze the *why* behind the numbers—what it was about that second video that drove more viewers to become paying customers.

With this knowledge in hand, you can better focus future videos to include the elements that made the second video more effective. And that's the key: To learn from what you've done to become more successful going forward.

The Big Picture

One of the great things about online videos is that it's easy to track how successful they are. YouTube includes a wealth of tools that tell you how many people viewed each video, how they found it, and how your videos compare to other videos on the site. You can supplement YouTube's statistics with data from your own website to judge which YouTube videos are driving the most traffic back to your site.

Ultimately, however, you want your YouTube videos to result in increased sales for your products and services. Tracking direct sales is easy enough (by embedding some sort of unique tracking code in each video) but almost impossible if your products are sold via traditional retail or wholesale channels. That said, you can get a hint of how well your videos work by talking directly with your customers via surveys and the like; you can gain much knowledge by simply asking your customers, "Have you seen our videos on YouTube?"

The point is to do more than just post videos on YouTube; you want to post *effective* videos. The only way to do that is to track each video's performance and learn from what you discover. Use all the tools at your disposal (from YouTube and other services) to gather all the data possible and then determine what makes one video more effective than another. That knowledge is power—and the way to make YouTube an even more effective part of your marketing mix. ∎

15

Promoting Your YouTube Videos

The best-made video on YouTube is a dismal failure if no one watches it. How do you attract viewers to your YouTube videos and thus create more potential customers for your business?

With millions of videos posted on the YouTube site, it's tough to get your content noticed. Fortunately, there are many different ways you can promote your YouTube videos to attract new viewers. We discuss some of the more effective ones in this chapter.

Start with Great Content...

It goes without saying that all the promotion in the world won't attract viewers to a video that doesn't offer some distinct value. Viewers who follow the promotion to a lousy video simply click the Stop button when they begin to get bored, which happens soon enough. It all starts with great content, which can benefit from additional promotion.

Entertain, Inform, or Educate

The best YouTube videos offer something valuable to viewers. I like to say that for a video to attract viewers, it has to do one of three things: entertain, inform, or educate the viewer. Here's what I mean:

- **Entertain**—Most videos on YouTube strive to be entertaining. Whether you're talking cute kittens, stupid human tricks, or wryly humorous vlog postings, the typical YouTube video contains some measure of entertainment value. This can also work for business videos; just as many of the most memorable television commercials are vastly entertaining (typically in a humorous vein), some of the most-viewed YouTube business videos are similarly entertaining. After all, people like to be entertained; if you can pull off such an entertaining video, it's bound to draw viewers.

- **Inform**—One other thing that attracts viewers is information—in particular, information that is specifically relevant and useful to the viewer. I'm talking about the latest news, tailor-made for the target YouTube customer. When your company video has information that matters to particular YouTube viewers, those people watch it.

- **Educate**—In a similar fashion, anytime you can help someone learn how to do something that they need to do, you attract eyeballs. Show mechanically inept viewers how to the change the oil in their cars or teach would-be chefs how to prepare a gourmet meal, and the help you provide gains praise. Step-by-step instruction attracts large numbers of viewers in today's increasingly do-it-yourself world—as witnessed by the success of HGTV and the Food Network on cable television.

Pick one approach—entertainment, information, or education—and do it as best you can. Provide stellar content, and you're well on your way to upping your video view count.

Target Your Content

Here's something else about the content of your videos: The more targeted it is, the faster it finds an audience. Yes, general videos would seem to appeal to a larger slice of the YouTube community, but general videos also get lost among the millions of other general videos; it's tough to stand out in a crowd this large.

A much better approach is to target a particular slice of the community—a distinct customer base. As in any other form of advertising, the more narrowly you target the message, the more appeal you have to those targeted consumers.

In addition, when you niche-target your content, you can more easily promote it via YouTube's community features, as well in the blogosphere and on social networks. When you narrowly identify the audience, it's a snap to locate the groups, blogs, forums, and other outlets that target the same audience. A broadly focused video is much more difficult to promote; there are just too many channels to choose from, none of which is an exact hit. In fact, a general interest video may reach an audience altogether different from the one you really want to reach. Why waste your time targeting viewers who will never be your customers? You can more effectively and efficiently promote a narrowly targeted video via channels narrowly targeted in the same way.

Optimize Your Tags

When it comes to making viewers aware of your videos, remember the tags—the keywords that viewers use to search for videos on YouTube. Without the right tags, great content will go unfound; add the appropriate tags, and you make it easier for viewers to find your videos.

To optimize the tags you apply to your video, you have to think like the customer. Get inside the heads of your potential customers and think how they might search for the information they need. When you figure out the keywords they'll most likely search for, you have the most effective tags for your video.

Your tags should include a combination of both generic and specific keywords. For example, if your video talks about the differences between incandescent and fluorescent lighting, you should include generic tags such as *lighting, light bulb, energy efficient*, and the like, as well as more specific tags such as *incandescent, fluorescent*, and *your company name*. In this way, you attract viewers that are essentially browsing or just getting interested in the topic, and make yourself known to those viewers that have more specific needs in mind or are searching specifically for your company.

Write a Compelling Title

The title of your video is crucial to attracting viewers. Not only is your title searched by YouTube when users submit queries, it's also how most viewers determine what your video is about.

Yes, the full description is there to read, but most people skim rather than read—especially when they're browsing through a page full of search results. So, your title has to not only include the most important keywords or tags, but also convey the content of the video.

That means, of course, that you have to create a concise, descriptive, and compelling title. It's copywriting at its finest, distilling the essence of what you have to offer in a short line of copy; it takes a lot of work and a lot of experience to get right.

Pick the Best Thumbnail Image

Finally, remember what a typical YouTube search results page looks like— lots of video listings, each accompanied by a single thumbnail image, as shown in Figure 15.1. You need to attract viewers to your specific listing in the search results, which means presenting the most attractive and relevant thumbnail image possible.

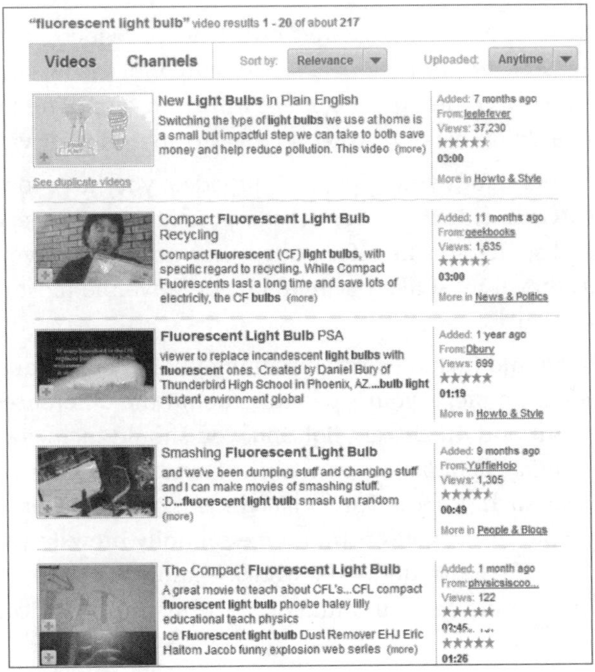

FIGURE 15.1

Optimize your thumbnail image to stand out on search results pages.

YouTube lets you choose from three possible images to use as your video's thumbnail image. It grabs the images from different points in your video. To choose a thumbnail image, click Account, My Videos to display your Videos page. Click the Edit Video Info button for the video you want to edit; when the Edit My Video page appears, as shown in Figure 15.2, click the image you want to use as your thumbnail.

FIGURE 15.2

Choosing an image to use for your video thumbnail.

> **tip**
>
> You don't have to keep the same thumbnail image forever. Many marketers switch thumbnail images over the course of a video's YouTube life, thus freshening the video's appearance on search results pages.

The best thumbnails are clear, not blurry, and have a dominant subject— ideally a person's face or a close-up of the product you're selling. You can also stand out from the other listings with a brightly colored or high-contrast image in your thumbnail—anything to make the thumbnail "pop" on the search results page.

Take Advantage of YouTube's Community Features

One of the best places to promote your YouTube video is on YouTube itself. When you make the YouTube community aware of what you're doing, other viewers do your promotion for you. Word-of-mouth marketing is alive and well on the YouTube site.

Sharing with Friends

Let's start with those users who subscribe to your video channel, as well as those who added you to their Friends list. How do you let these positively predisposed viewers know that you have a new video to watch?

Dealing with subscribers is easy: YouTube does the work for you. Whenever you post a new video to the YouTube site, YouTube automatically sends an email to all of your channel's subscribers informing them of the video. That's easy.

More work is necessary to notify your friends of your latest video. Go to the video page, select the Share tab (under the video player), and click the Email link. This expands the tab to display the Send a Message area, as shown in Figure 15.3. To send a message to all your contacts, click the Add All link in the scrolling list. Enter your message (something along the lines of "Check out our latest video") in the Message box and click the Send button.

FIGURE 15.3
Sending an email to your YouTube friends.

Your friends receive an email message like the one in Figure 15.4. To view your video, all they have to do is click the video thumbnail or the Watch Video link; doing so takes them to the video page on the YouTube site, and you have one new viewer.

Broadcasting Bulletins

Here's another way to send a message about a new video to your Friends list as well as to anyone viewing your YouTube channel page. It involves sending a bulletin, via email, which contains a link to your video of choice.

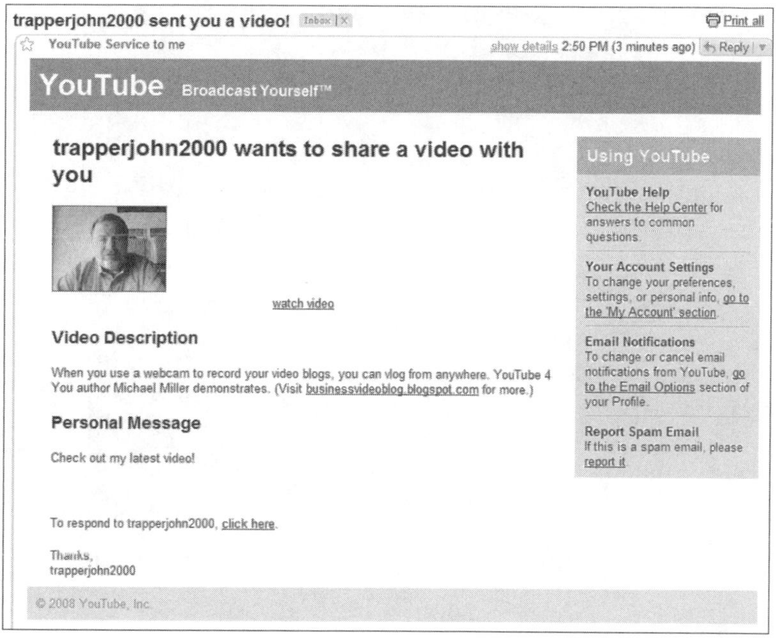

FIGURE 15.4

The email that your friends receive.

To send a bulletin, go to your channel page, scroll to the Bulletins box, and click the Broadcast a Message link. This displays the Bulletin Post page, shown in Figure 15.5. As you can see, you don't have to fill in the recipient's list; YouTube does it for you. All you have to do is enter a subject for the message, write a message in the Body box, and select the video you want to feature (from the pull-down Attach a Video list). When you finish doing this, click the Post Bulletin button.

YouTube emails your bulletin to everyone on your Friends list and posts it to the Bulletins section of your channel page. When visitors click the link for this bulletin, they see the page shown in Figure 15.6. To view the video, all they have to do is click the thumbnail image.

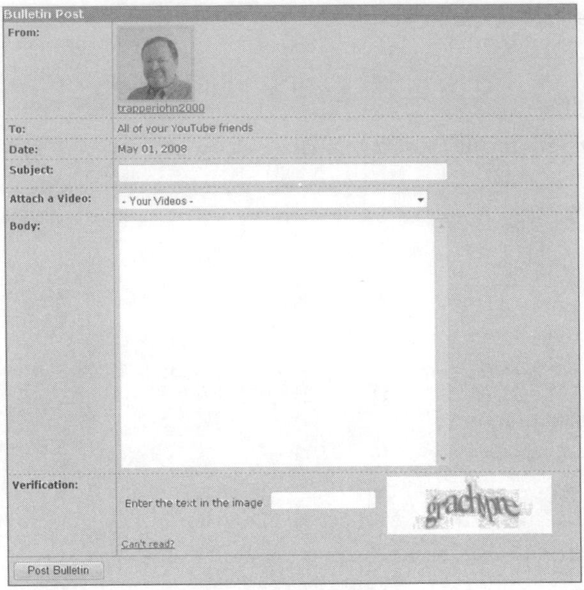

FIGURE 15.5

Creating a bulletin for your friends and your channel page.

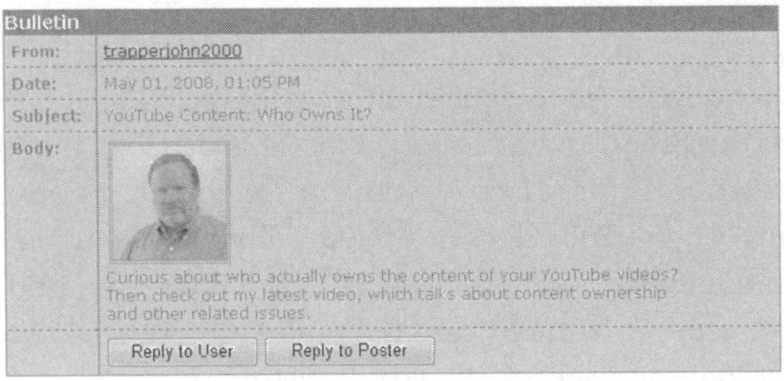

FIGURE 15.6

A bulletin that announces your latest video.

note

Learn more about YouTube's community features in Chapter 10, "Creating a YouTube Presence."

Use Email Marketing

Of course, you're not limited to promoting your videos to the YouTube community. You can also promote your videos to anyone else on or off the Web.

One of the best ways to do this is to create an email mailing list on your main website, typically populated with email addresses provided by your customers. When you post a new video to YouTube, send a mailing to the entire list, letting your customers know all about the video and including a link to the video on YouTube. You might be surprised at how effective this simple technique can be.

caution

Your email mailing list needs to be an opt-in list, or you may be accused of sending spam to your valued customers.

Reach Out to the Blogosphere

You can drive a lot of traffic to a YouTube video by getting that video mentioned on relevant blogs. It requires a bit of work to identify the blogs that might be interested in the content of your video, but then it's a simple matter of sending out a press release (via email) that describes the video and includes a link to the YouTube video page. You might even want to include your video's embed code in the introductory email, in case the blogger wants to actually embed your video in his blog.

tip

If you're so inclined, and have the time, you can reach out to individual bloggers via personal emails. This hands-on approach is much more effective than the blanket press release method.

In some instances, you might be able to pay bloggers to mention your videos. This pay per post (PPP) approach seems odious to some, but it's increasingly common in the blogosphere. If you're unfamiliar with the practice, you might want to check out Blogitive (www.blogitive.com), a company that helps businesses build a buzz by placing paid posts with a large network of sympathetic bloggers.

When a blogger links to or embeds your video in his blog, you just created a new stream of viewers for your video. A certain percentage of these new viewers link back to your corporate website, just as a certain percentage subscribe to your channel to view future videos—thus becoming future potential customers.

Post to Other Web Forums

Along the same lines, you should work the various websites, forums, and message boards that target the same audience as your videos. Participate in appropriate discussions on these forums so that you can throw in a mention of or link to your video without appearing particularly mercenary.

After you become a familiar face on a given forum, it's okay to start a new discussion when you have a new video to promote. Yes, this is a tedious and time-consuming approach, but it's quite effective; you're reaching out to some of the most influential members of the target community.

caution

In most web communities, don't even think about making a promotional post until you've established a presence in the community. Most communities are quite insular and uniformly dismissive of "carpetbaggers" operating purely in their own self-interest.

Work the Social Networks

Another way to drive traffic to your videos is via a presence on Facebook, MySpace, and similar social networks. After you create your own personal or company page on these websites, you can embed videos on it.

In fact, YouTube makes it easy to send videos to both Facebook and MySpace. All you have to do is select the Share tab under the video player on the video page and then click either the Facebook or MySpace icon. When you click the Facebook icon, you see the window shown in Figure 15.7.

Enter a comment in the box and click the Post button, and your Facebook profile adds the video, as shown in Figure 15.8.

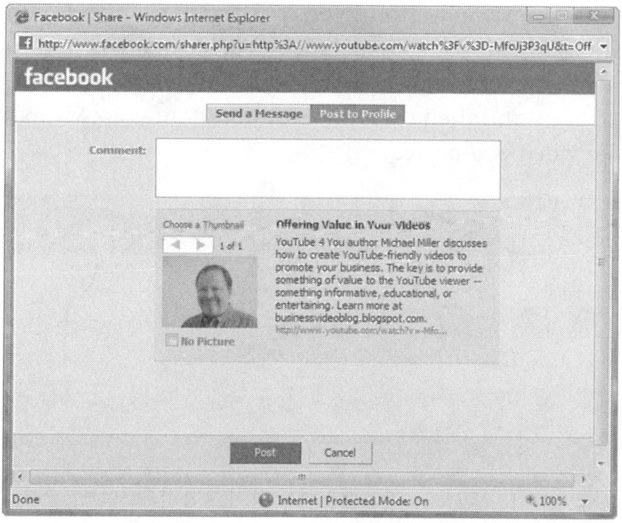

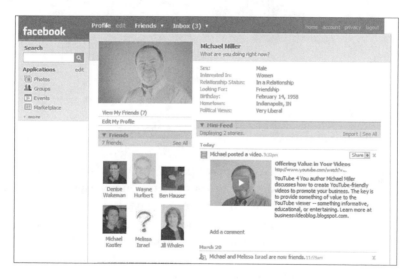

FIGURE 15.7

Posting a video to your Facebook profile.

FIGURE 15.8

A Facebook profile with a YouTube video added.

If you click the MySpace icon, you move to the confirmation page shown in Figure 15.9. Edit the subject line, select a category from the pull-down list, and enter a short description in the Body box. Select any other appropriate options and then click the Post It button; your MySpace blog displays the video you posted.

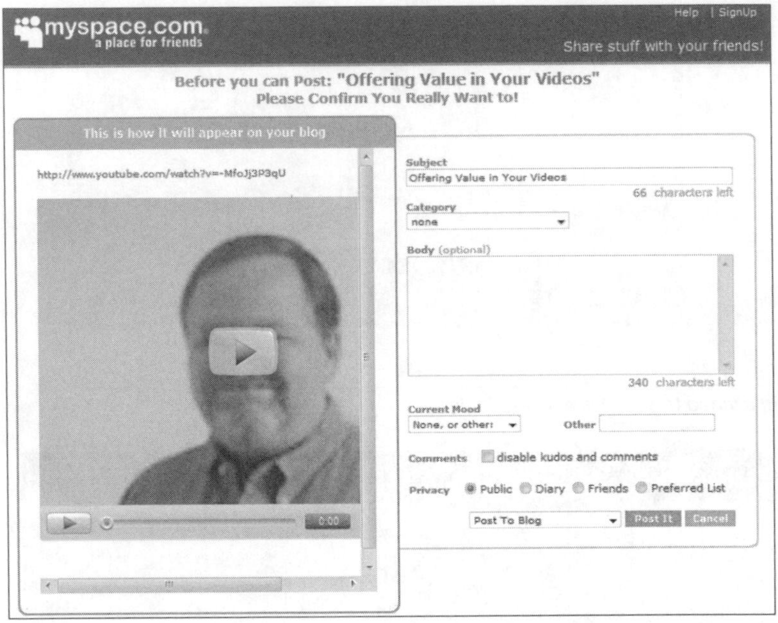

FIGURE 15.9

Posting a video to your MySpace blog.

In addition to posting to your own pages, you can share your videos with your friends on both these sites. For example, many MySpace users let you embed YouTube videos into the comments section of their pages. Facebook enables you to share a video with everyone on your friends list. The takeaway is that you should take advantage of all the features of the major social networking sites to promote your video with the widest possible network of online friends and acquaintances.

tip

You should also promote your video on social news sites such as Digg (www.digg.com) and StumbleUpon (www.stumbleupon.com). When you post a link to your video on these sites, it will be discovered by a wide range of other users—thus broadening the viewership of your video.

Run a Contest

Here's a method mentioned elsewhere in the book but worth repeating here. One interesting way to draw viewers to your videos is to run a contest of some sort. Some of the most successful contests directly involve viewers with the company's videos by encouraging them to remix existing videos or create their own videos for the company or product.

Naturally, some customers will be attracted by any prizes you dole out, but most will visit your channel or group just to see what other YouTubers are posting; contest entries are bound to be entertaining in any number of ways. The most creative viewers will post entries to the contest—some of which might be good enough for you to use in other media. It's a win-win for you because you get a spike in viewership, attract new customers, and reinforce your bonds with your existing customer base.

Promote Traditionally

Although our focus is primarily on the Web, we mustn't neglect more traditional forms of promotion—including old-fashioned PR. That means issuing paper (and electronic) press releases, as well as picking up the phone (or firing up the email program) to hand-target individual publications and news outlets.

For example, if you have a video that has particular relevance to a particular industry, you can reach out to industry trade groups, publications, and the like with news about your video. Make sure you include a link to (or the URL for) the video in your press release, of course; any online news source can link directly from its coverage to the video on the YouTube site.

Likewise, if your video is of local or regional interest, reach out to your local news organizations—newspapers, television stations, radio stations, and their online arms. The best of all possible worlds comes when your video is not only mentioned on a local newscast, but also shown on air!

Upload to Other Video-Sharing Sites

One last thing: You shouldn't limit your video to only YouTube. There are lots of other video-sharing sites on the Web. Although the other sites are smaller than the YouTube community, they can help expand the reach of your video. Some of those sites are

- AOL Uncut Video (uncutvideo.aol.com)
- blip.tv (www.blip.tv)
- Dailymotion (www.dailymotion.com)
- Flixya (www.flixya.com)
- GUBA (www.guba.com)
- Jumpcut (www.jumpcut.com)
- Metacafe (www.metacafe.com)
- Ourmedia (www.ourmedia.org)
- Revver (www.revver.com)
- Sharkle (www.sharkle.com)
- Veoh (www.veoh.com)
- Vimeo (www.vimeo.com)
- vSocial (www.vsocial.com)
- Yahoo! Video (video.yahoo.com)
- YouAreTV (www.youare.tv)
- ZippyVideos (www.zippyvideos.com)

> **note**
>
> Even with all these competitors, YouTube remains the big dog. Most research puts YouTube's market share as larger than all its rivals—combined!

Obviously, you should include your video on your own company website. Your site has lots of visitors that might never visit the YouTube site; give them the opportunity to view your videos without leaving your official site!

The Big Picture

You can't just upload a video to the YouTube site and expect a thousand views overnight. It takes a lot of hard work and creativity to attract viewers to your videos; it doesn't happen by chance.

If you're lucky, all your effort results in an upsurge of viewers for your video. At this point, success begins to beget success. That is, the more viewers you attract, the more they talk about and recommend your video, thus further increasing the view count. You need viewers to create more viewers.

Then, if you're even luckier, your video's view count is high enough to become one of YouTube's top-rated videos. When this happens, your video appears on YouTube's Videos tab, which displays the daily most-viewed videos. This is when your video hits the big time; with this type of prominent exposure, you get even more views than you did before. As I said, success begets success.

From there, the next logical step is to go viral. This happens when your video's viewership expands beyond YouTube. Maybe a local television station picks up the video, or you get a mention on a major website, or CNN or MSNBC—or even David Letterman or *The Daily Show*—start showing the video on the home screen. If you're lucky enough for this to happen, get ready for a wild ride. Your view count could easily hit the seven figure mark, and you can get more buzz than you ever thought possible.

This, of course, is what we all strive for: massive exposure with minimal cost and effort. But both you and I know that the effort wasn't minimal; you have to work hard just to get basic exposure for your video, let alone go viral. ■

16

Generating Revenues from Your YouTube Videos

By this point in reading this book, you're no doubt convinced of the value of adding YouTube videos to your online marketing mix. But how, exactly, can you turn those videos into cash? How can you monetize the YouTube channel?

Of course, not all marketing activities have to result directly in sales; some activities exist purely to build or enhance the brand. You can generate revenues from your YouTube videos in a number of ways; we look at a few in this chapter.

Directly Selling Products and Services

Probably the most common way to realize the revenue-generating potential of a YouTube video is to use it to drive direct sales of your company's products or services. The goal is to convert viewers into paying customers as quickly and as directly as possible.

Doing so requires a three-step process. First, you have to create a video with unique value, something that attracts viewers. Second, that video has to effectively (if subtly) promote your product and direct potential customers to your regular website. Last, your website has to offer your product or service for sale, enabling interested customers to finalize the purchase.

Let's look at all three steps.

Create a Video with Value

Not to flog a deceased *Equus caballus*, but the first step in any marketing-related activity on YouTube is to create a video that viewers actually want to watch. As I hope you've already learned, there are three ways to do this:

- Create an *entertaining* video—People love to laugh.
- Create an *informative* video—People like to get the latest news.
- Create an *educational* video—People need to learn how to do certain things.

If your video neither entertains, informs, nor educates, people won't watch it. That's the bottom line.

In all three instances, note that your video is *not* an overt advertisement for what you're selling. That's something else YouTubers won't watch: blatant commercials. They get enough commercials on regular television; they don't want to waste their Internet bandwidth watching more of the same. This is why your video has to attract attention through its subject matter; a commercial message doesn't have that type of valuable content.

So, work hard to produce a video that interests potential buyers of your product or service. Get inside your customers' heads and find out what they want to see. It might be something entertaining, it might be a bit of valuable information, or it might be a useful step-by-step how-to. In any case, you have to start with compelling content; anything less and your entire marketing plan falls apart.

Direct Viewers to Your Website

When you produce a video designed to directly sell a product, you need to incorporate selling pointers throughout the video. Think of your video as one of those late-night infomercials; yes, they're (sporadically) entertaining, but they also make it easy for you to place an order.

How do you including selling pointers in your video? Here are some of the most common approaches:

- Include the URL of your website (or a toll-free telephone number) upfront, in the title card for the video. The title card could also include the price of the product, any special offers, and other ordering instructions.
- Add a credits card at the end of the video, also with complete ordering instructions.

- If the video is a longer one (more than 2–3 minutes in length), superimpose your website URL or phone number onscreen over the course of the video.

- For longer videos, consider inserting a break somewhere in the middle that features a direct call to action by some onscreen personality—kind of like a PBS pledge break.

- Incorporate a subtle selling pitch in the script of the video, much the same way infomercial "hosts" plug their products as part of the onscreen presentation.

In other words, don't be afraid to talk about purchasing your product, but don't let the sales pitch get in the way of the content presentation. Suggest the sale, but subtly.

You should also include a sales pitch and ordering information in the video's text description. Don't make the viewer rewatch the entire video when they want to place an order!

tip

Make sure you include ordering information on your main channel page, as well.

Close the Sale on Your Website

Now it's time to close the sale, which, because you can't sell directly from your YouTube page, you do on your own website. The URL you point to from your YouTube video should be a relatively hard-sell landing page. That means that you don't point to a generic page on your site or even to your site's home page; both approaches require unnecessary work on the part of the customer to place an order. Instead, link to a specific product page on your site, one that includes information about only the product shown in the video.

Why design a special landing page for viewers of your YouTube video? It's simple: You want to make it as easy as possible for them to give you their money. If you just dump potential customers on your site's home page, they could get lost. Or they might have trouble finding the product they want and give up. In any instance, you don't want them randomly browsing your site; you want them immediately responding to your specific offer.

For this reason, your product landing page should have the same look and feel of the video so that viewers sense the underlying connection. It doesn't hurt to include a screenshot or two from the video, or even an embedded version of the video in case the customer wants to rewatch it. The page should also include more detailed information about the product than was possible in the video, as well as more detailed product photos.

> **note**
>
> The *landing page* is the page that appears when a potential customer clicks an advertisement or search engine results link. This page should display content that is a logical extension of the advertisement or link. Depending on the nature and intent of the page, it should provide additional information, ask for information from the customer, or ask for the sale.

Some experts recommend a more stripped-down landing page, with links to additional information if the customer needs it. The thinking is that anyone clicking to this page has already been convinced to buy; you don't want to introduce any element that might make her rethink her decision.

In any case, the most important element on the product landing page is the click-to-order button. Don't make the customer do a lot of work; make it easy to click one button to initiate the order process.

When the customer clicks the order button, she can move to your site's normal shopping cart or checkout section. For tracking purposes, make sure that you credit to your YouTube video any orders flowing from the specific product landing page.

> **tip**
>
> Don't forget to suggest add-on or accessory sales to your new customer—ideally on the page immediately following the initial product landing page.

Selling Advertising Around Embedded Videos on Your Own Website

Not all marketers seek to create direct sales from their YouTube videos; many companies prefer to drive sales through their established retail and wholesale channels. There is still a way for these companies to generate revenues from their YouTube videos—by using those videos as unique online advertising vehicles. All you need is your YouTube video, your own website or blog, and a subscription to Google AdSense or a similar advertising service.

Embedding Videos on Your Website

The key to this approach is to generate revenues from your own website or blog, from traffic driven by embedded YouTube videos. The most interesting your videos, the more traffic you attract; the more traffic you attract, the more click-throughs you get on the ads you place on your site.

---

tip

This approach isn't limited to just your own videos. You can embed *any* YouTube video on your website and use that video to generate advertising revenues!

This approach is simplicity itself. All you have to do is embed your own YouTube video somewhere on your website or blog, using the embed code that YouTube creates for all of its videos. As noted earlier in this book, you don't actually host the video on your website; YouTube provides the hosting and bandwidth. Your involvement is nothing more than cutting and pasting a few lines of code into your site's underlying HTML.

Adding Click-Through Advertising

What you do next, of course, is what generates the revenues. You surround the embedded video on your site with click-through advertising, such as that shown in Figure 16.1. When a visitor to your site clicks on the link in the ad, you receive a small fee. The more clicks, the more money you earn. For ads surrounding a high-popularity video, the revenue can be substantial.

FIGURE 16.1

A typical block of click-through ads from Google AdSense.

Of course, this approach involves signing up for some sort of ad revenue-sharing service, the most popular being AdSense, which just happens to be owned by Google, the company that owns YouTube. (You might as well keep it all in the family—especially because AdSense is so easy to use.)

Using Google AdSense

Google's AdSense program places content-targeted ads on your site, sells those ads to appropriate advertisers, monitors visitor click-throughs, tracks how much money you have coming, and then pays you what you've earned. All you have to do is sign up for the program, insert a few lines of code into your web page's underlying HTML code, and sit back and let Google do the rest of the work.

Because AdSense ads are context-sensitive, the ads served should relate to the content of your videos. For example, if you embed a how-to video that shows how to connect a computer printer, AdSense might serve up an ad for printers or ink cartridges. It shouldn't be jarring to your site's visitors.

caution

The only caveat to placing AdSense ads on your own website is that you might end up with ads from your competitors. Of course, you make money from any customers clicking away to your competitor's site, but it's still not something some companies are comfortable with.

Signing up for the Google AdSense program is easy enough to do and completely free. You start at the main AdSense page (www.google.com/adsense/), shown in Figure 16.2, and then click the Click Here to Apply button. The next page is an application form; fill it in and then let Google review your application. The review period typically runs two to three days. Google notifies you of your acceptance, and you're ready to log in to your AdSense account and get started with the rest of the process.

After Google approves your account, you need to insert ads into your website. To do this, go to the AdSense home page, click the AdSense for Content link, and then select what type of ad (size and format) you want to insert. Google displays the HTML code for the ad; copy and paste this code into the HTML code for your web page. Your page now displays the ad block, with ad content relevant to the YouTube video you've also embedded on the page.

You make money anytime someone clicks the links in the ad. AdSense keeps track of all clicks and issues checks, or deposits to your bank account, on a monthly basis.

note

Clickers don't have to purchase anything from the advertiser for you to generate revenues from your ads. AdSense operates purely on a pay-per-click basis.

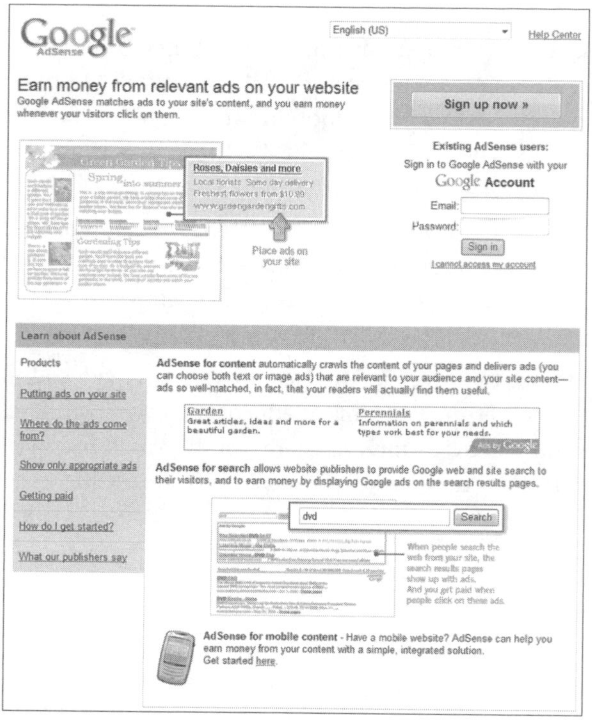

FIGURE 16.2

Use Google AdSense to generate revenues from YouTube videos embedded in your website.

The Big Picture

Given that you can't sell products directly from your YouTube videos, there are ways to use those videos to generate revenues. For many sellers, the right approach is to direct customers from your video to a product landing page on your own website. This lets you convert viewers to purchasers—and you get to keep all the revenue! The key is to create a video that combines valuable content with a subtle selling message, much the way a good infomercial does; just make sure you include lots of pointers from your video (and its text description) to your website's URL.

Another approach is to embed your YouTube video on your own web page and then sell advertising on that page. Some percentage of viewers will click the links in the ads, and you get cash for each click-through. The easiest way to do this is with Google AdSense, although several online advertising services offer similar pay-per-click advertising.

Of course, not all companies want or need their YouTube videos to generate direct revenue. The best company videos work to build the company's brand and provide added promotion for the products and services the company sells. That's the magic of YouTube; with every viewer, you broaden your customer base. And it all happens at a relatively low cost.

That combination of efficiency and effectiveness makes YouTube an ideal marketing channel for even the smallest companies. In fact, YouTube is a great equalizer; a little guy can easily compete with the big guys without going broke.

Just remember to think like the customer. Create videos that offer unique value—that entertain, inform, or educate. Viewers will flock to useful and entertaining videos, as long as there's no hard sell involved. Offer value and sell subtly; that's the key to YouTube business success! ■

YouTube BUSINESS PROFILE

Profile: D-Link

Company Profile

Company: D-Link

Product: Networking equipment

YouTube channel: www.youtube.com/user/DLinkTV

Websites: www.dlinktv.com, www.dlink.com

D-Link Meets the Web

To demonstrate that YouTube is an ideal marketing vehicle for companies of all sizes, let's look at one of the biggest companies using YouTube today. D-Link is probably familiar to most readers, being one of the industry's largest manufacturers of networking equipment. The company produces routers and wireless adapters and all the pieces and parts you need to put together a home or business network.

D-Link uses online videos on a number of sites to promote its full line of products. YouTube is just one of the channels for D-Link's videos, dubbed D-LinkTV; the company also hosts its own D-LinkTV website and puts its videos on a host of partner sites.

How did D-Link get the idea for its D-LinkTV videos? According to Daniel Kelley, senior director of Marketing, the company recognized in the market a need for customers to learn more about D-Link's products and to learn how to use them. As Daniel admits, networking products can sometimes be complicated, even though D-Link works on engineering them for the customer. The company's first step is getting the consumer to understand what the product does and making that customer feel comfortable making a purchase. Industry trends show that streaming video on the Web was becoming more accepted and popular, especially with the widespread adoption of broadband and improved streaming technology, so company management knew it was a type of media it could leverage.

The D-LinkTV website.

The first video D-Link shot was an informational video on the need to secure a home network. But that was just the tip of the iceberg. When the D-LinkTV site officially launched in February 2007, it had more than 50 videos available.

Why so many videos at the start? As Daniel notes, "It went live with so many videos to get a competitive start on other competitors in the market. We knew we were taking a risk but we were also trying to take a leadership in the industry of video tech help."

Those first videos garnered big viewership and acceptance and, equally important, got widespread press coverage. D-Link had accomplished its goal: immediate recognition as a leader in this type of content. And that press coverage resulted in even more viewers, with a spike in viewership levels after the first month or so, and continual growth in viewership thereafter.

YouTube as Part of the Online Marketing Mix

As I mentioned, D-Link displays its videos not just on YouTube but also on its own corporate website. D-Link also has its videos on the sites of many of its largest retail partners, including TigerDirect (www.tigerdirect.com), Buy.com (www.buy.com), Costco (www.costco.com), and Best Buy (www.bestbuy.com). Dan notes that they receive a lot of views on these partner sites "because customers can watch a video before actually buying the product."

A D-Link video included on a product information page on the TigerDirect website.

Of all these sites, the most important is the company's own corporate website, which is where consumers and business owners tend to go for product information. It's also the most logical place to host and promote the company's videos.

That said, Dan says that putting all the company's videos on YouTube "was a great business plan, because of the potential for viral sharing of these videos from person to person." He goes on to note that viewership has increased steadily due to reviews coming from YouTube and other social networking sites: "Sites like YouTube really hold the potential for any video to take off and become widespread, due to accessibility of the Internet around the world."

Impacting Sales

D-LinkTV is not a small endeavor. As of May 2008, D-Link had produced more than 260 videos. They receive 5,000 to 10,000 views per day on the corporate website, with viewership on YouTube and other partner sites being somewhat more difficult to track.

How have all these videos and viewers affected the company's sales? As Dan admits, "It's hard to tell, because you cannot track a connection between someone watching a video and then going out and buying the product. But as far as feedback goes, we have seen many emails and positive feedback based on the videos. Emails including statements like 'I'll never buy a non–D-Link brand again' are common. These videos show us that we are building good customer loyalty due to the helpfulness of the videos."

Different Types of Videos

One of the keys to D-LinkTV is that the company doesn't just produce one type of video. Instead, it produces product videos, Q&A videos, D.I.Y. (do-it-yourself) videos, and so forth. Of all these videos, Dan says that the product videos are the most popular:

We believe this is because people are more careful about the product they buy. When they are making a purchase of $100 or more they do their research to make sure they are getting the most and best for their money. The product videos are great research for consumers because it is a media they are very comfortable [with]. The popularity of television and YouTube shows that people like to see what the product can do and see a person interacting with the product before they go out and buy it.

A typical D-LinkTV product video—that's Dan Kelley onscreen.

Dan goes on to note that the company has also received good feedback on its D.I.Y. videos. These release weekly and because of the helpful content shown in a comfortable environment, they are positively accepted.

Bottom line, D-Link uses its videos for education, to inform customers about its products, and to benefit its customers via helpful information about D-Link products. That makes D-LinkTV a big part of D-Link's marketing mix, especially with new products; the videos help generate publicity about what the product does and how it works.

Advice for Other Businesses

Like most businesses using online video to promote their businesses, D-Link's videos started out rather inexpensive at the beginning, with minimal investment in equipment. However, given the aggressive schedule of new videos, the company is investing more and more in video production, to the point of having built two studios in the company's main building. D-Link also updated its equipment to include HDTV cameras. That said, the biggest part of the budget is personnel, which is difficult to put a price on per video. The company uses almost exclusively D-Link employees on camera.

Even with that investment in equipment and personnel, D-Link has learned over time that more relaxed, impromptu videos do better than tightly scripted ones; the more unscripted the video, the better it comes across. As Dan Kelley notes:

In the beginning, we were trying to script every sentence and it came off too scripted. Now we use bullet points to make it more casual and personal. We also have expanded the large range of videos that we do. We have learned that the need for YouTube is entertainment and funnier videos. The dry informational videos on products are not as popular as the more 'infotainment' ones. The more entertaining and exciting the better the video and the more views we receive.

Dan also has this advice for other businesses seeking to make online videos part of their marketing mix:

You need to get the videos up and make them part of your normal marketing plan, because you never know what the response to a certain video will be. There are great opportunities to share and make videos that are very helpful. Don't overlook YouTube because it gets a ton of hits on a website separate from your own—which can help even the smallest business.

Good advice from a marketer benefiting hugely from YouTube and the online video revolution. Can you match D-Link's success?

Index

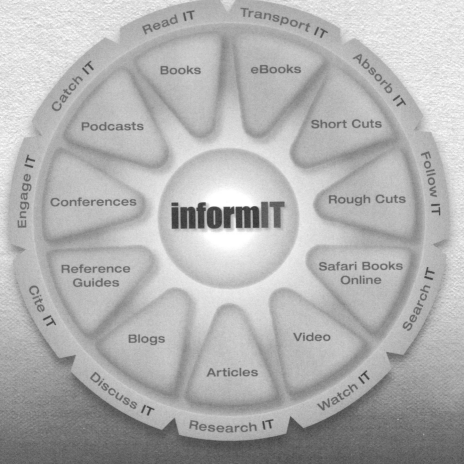

YouTube for Business
Online Video Marketing for Any Business

"Never thought you could use YouTube for your business? Well, think again! This book gives you a complete overview of why, how, and the technology to get you started."
— Rhonda Abrams, USAToday small business columnist and author of *Successful Marketing Secrets & Strategies*

FREE Online Edition

Your purchase of *YouTube for Business: Online Video Marketing for Any Business* includes access to a free online edition for 45 days through the Safari Books Online subscription service. Nearly every Que book is available online through Safari Books Online, along with over 5,000 other technical books and videos from publishers such as Addison-Wesley Professional, Cisco Press, Exam Cram, IBM Press, O'Reilly, Prentice Hall, and Sams.

SAFARI BOOKS ONLINE allows you to search for a specific answer, cut and paste code, download chapters, and stay current with emerging technologies.

Activate your FREE Online Edition at
www.informit.com/safarifree

> **STEP 1:** Enter the coupon code: SZL4-I4NM-LBGV-3UM3-KPPE.

> **STEP 2:** New Safari users, complete the brief registration form.
> Safari subscribers, just login.

If you have difficulty registering on Safari or accessing the online edition, please e-mail customer-service@safaribooksonline.com

Safari
Books Online